FITRA JOURNAL:
THE MUSLIM HOMESCHOOL QUARTERLY

First Edition, 2016

Copyright 2016 Fitra Journal
www.fitrajournal.com
Editor: Brooke Benoit

Design by Reyhana Ismail
www.reyoflightdesign.com

All rights reserved. No part of this publication may be reproduced in any language, stored in any retrieval system or transmitted in any form or by any means - electronic, mechanical, photocopying, recording or otherwise - without the express permission of the copyright owner.

CONTENTS

Dealing with Devices: Brooke Benoit..4

CHAPTER 1: BEGINNINGS...7
Building Bonds and Boundaries - Establishing Solid Foundational Relationships with Our Children: Khalida Haque..8
Home to School and Back Again: Karrie Chariton...13
An Unexpected Journey to Homeschooling My Children: Omaira Alam............................17
A Mother's Lap is a Child's First School: Zawjah Ali..19
'Deschooling' 101: Zakiya Mahomed-Kalla..22

CHAPTER 2: HOMESCHOOLING IN THE DIGITAL AGE......................................25
Are You a Digital Immigrant or Digital Native?: Sumaia b. Michel....................................26
Technology: Necessary and Not so Bad at All: Sumaia b. Michel......................................27
Guiding Our Children on the Internet: Shaykh Ismail Kamdar..29
Raising a Reader Among Viewers: Asma Ali..32
Creating an IT Study Unit for Screen-free Children: Klaudia Khan...................................36
Best Practices for Technology in Home Education: Interview with Dr. Alan Fortescue By Brooke Benoit 38

CHAPTER 3: THEORY, METHOD AND STYLE..43
How to Enjoy Worldschooling at Home: Omaira Alam...44
One Teacher Finds his Calling in Homeschooling: Khadijah Hayley..................................48
"Aha!" Moments - The Hidden Blessings of Unschooling: Sadaf Farooqi..........................50
One Student's Pros and Cons List of Homeschooling: Faiza Rahhali................................54
Wavering Between University and Islamic Studies: Alexandria Potter..............................55
A Homeschooler's Hand in the Birth Campaign for Syrian Refugees: Isra Arfeen............58

CHAPTER 4: RESOURCES WE LOVE..61
Curriculum Review - BEarthschooling Institute: Chantal Blake...62
Curriculum Review - Oak Meadow: Shannon Staloch...64
Suggestions to Get Outside - with a Book or Two: Klaudia Khan.....................................66
Compilation of IT Studies Materials: Klaudia Khan...69

Our Contributors..70

Editorial: Dealing with Devices

Brooke Benoit

During this Ramadan our 'family' Kindle gave up on us. Being that this is our second Kindle which my kids have run into the ground, you may expect me to be fairly upset but instead I am relieved. It's not just that the kids need a break - I need a break! It feels like my children are either constantly on screens or plotting how to get on one as soon as possible. Screen usage wasn't always like this for my family; at the beginning of our homeschooling journey I felt that I was using technology wisely and responsibly.

I avoided electronic (noise and light-flashing) toys for my first born, opting for natural materials and open-ended play toys instead. I continue this practice today with my one year old. My older children groan about how they had the first Play Station console for years, and didn't even know it was a Play Station because we only had an educational reading game for it. Eventually they did begin gaming on our PC in the kitchen and this almost immediately initiated the battle of wills with me always wanting them to game less/study more and the children, of course, wanting the opposite ratio. The one thing I felt we did best was that the monitor was in the main room of the house. This is standard advice given about children and screen usage - not just to monitor their behavior, but so they can self-monitor. People (including children) generally don't want to put up something on the screen that they wouldn't want to be seen viewing, and sneakiness is greatly discouraged by monitors in shared space.

When we moved from the US to Morocco I bought our first Kindle as that seemed like the easiest way to acquire books for all of us. My older children were initially allowed to read books on the Kindle, but they very quickly were more enticed by the gaming apps and internet access. They now had a handheld device. This was a whole new game! It took me some time to figure out all of the device's parental controls, but there were and are still the battles over time and general access.

Soon after moving, my eldest bought his first handheld device, paying for it himself, at 14 years old. My 4 year old (and all my other kids!) saw herself as his equal. If he could have his own device, why couldn't she have the Kindle whenever she wanted? I feel like technology is a constant *fitna* (trial) in my homeschooling household, but if I set it aside and look at the rest of our lives, well it isn't any more so than the other things I struggle with - my children's diets, who they are playing with, their lack of motivation, fighting amongst themselves and so on. It's just another thing to worry about, and I do.

While I still think it's best to keep young children from screen time (and as you will read in my interview later in this issue, the American Academy of Pediatrics agrees), at some point we must learn how to best let our children learn to use digital technology and especially the internet. Klaudia Khan's approach, detailed in this issue, is absolutely brilliant and one I had never considered! Ultimately, as Shaykh Ismail Kamdar says in his article, just as we must teach our children to act responsibly in life - we must teach them to do the same online. In sha Allah, I hope this issue of *Fitra Journal* will help you find comfort and solutions for how to best use technology in your homeschool process. I for one am so happy to have this unplanned, unscheduled, unnegotiated unplugging. And no, they can't use my phone!

Thanks so much to all the contributors in this issue, their combined knowledge and experience is - *subhanAllah*! I hope to see you here in the fall when we will be talking about everyone's biggest concern - *but what about university?*

Brooke Benoit, Founding Editor of *Fitra Journal* | editor@fitrajournal.com

Chapter 1
BEGINNINGS

Building Bonds and Boundaries
Establishing Solid Foundational Relationships with Our Children

By Khalida Haque

"Having children makes you no more a parent than having a piano makes you a pianist."
- Michael Levine

o relationship just happens, even the ones with our children. And to develop any form of relationship means an investment of time, effort, and understanding. In the context of learning and teaching, it is essential and foundational that positive and healthy relationships are established with young children.

When does a Relationship with Our Children Start?
"The most important thing a father can do for his children is to love their mother, and the most important thing a mother can do for her children is to love their father." - Anonymous

To answer this question, I would suggest that we first look at an athar (saying) of Umar Ibn Al-Khattab (RA):
A man once came to him complaining of his son's disobedience. 'Umar called for the boy and asked him about his father's complaint, and his neglect of his duties towards his father. The boy replied, 'Does the child not have rights over his father?' 'Certainly' 'Umar replied. 'What are they then?' the boy asked. '*He should choose a mother with care, preferring the righteous woman. He should give his child a good name and teach him the Qur'an.*' 'O caliph! My father did none of these.' 'Umar turned to the father and said, 'You have come to complain about the disobedience of your son. You have failed in your duty to him before he failed in his duty to you. You wronged him before he wronged you.'

When we are choosing our spouses, our focus tends to be *what can this person do for me* and perhaps *will my family and friends like him/her*. We are caught up in the present, the things that matter right now. Being 'in the here and now' is very important; however, if it is preventing us from seeing the potential future impact of what is occurring in that precise moment then we can expect the unexpected. We rarely at the time of spouse-seeking consider that we are choosing a parent for our future children. And if that is an *amanah* (a trust) that we are blessed with, then we should recognize just how essential that consideration is.

This saying also clarifies for us our children's rights over us. All too often I hear parents insisting that a child respect them or that they be kind to them. After all parents have that right, right? But how are we behaving with that child?

"We can improve our relationships with others by leaps and bounds if we become encouragers instead of critics." - Joyce Meyer

Primarily we learn our parenting from our parents. We may not be consciously making notes but unconsciously as we grow we internalise (that is, we imbibe and absorb) the way that our parents relate with us. Utilising computing parlance, they are writing a default position program on our hard drive which will be triggered by the right (or wrong - depending on how you view things) conditions. Without a doubt, during our upbringings there are things we have categorically told ourselves that we will not do as parents. Realistically we do not consciously know what we have stored within us until we get into this relationship, unless we have been thoughtful and reflective and, perhaps, engaged in some psychotherapy/psychotherapeutic intervention. However, then the true litmus test of what is within us is the parent-child relationship.

To me, real and effective parenting is being good at relationships. And to be good at relationships you have got to accept yourself and who you are as well as allow the other person to be an individual and who they are.

Maslow's Hierachy of Needs
"There are two things we should give our children: one is roots and the other is wings." - Unknown

Below is a pictorial depiction of Maslow's hierarchy of human needs:

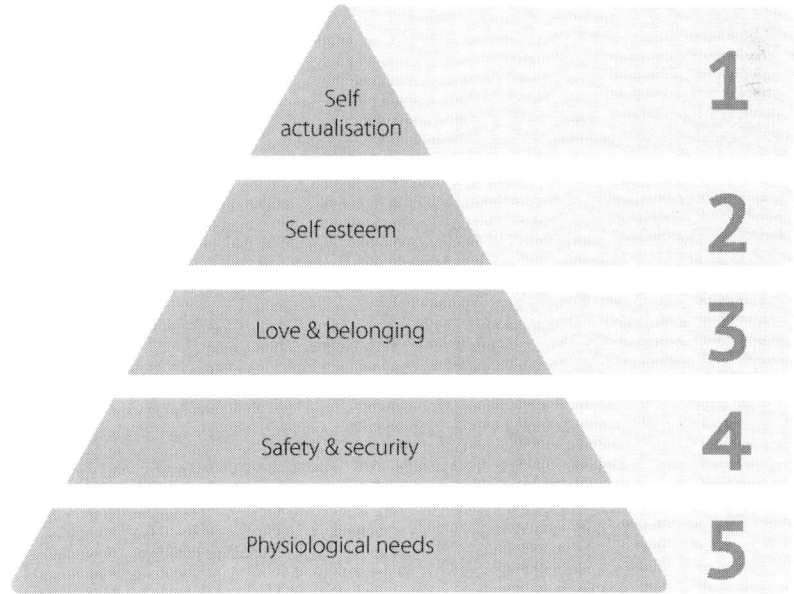

Abraham Maslow (died 1970) was one of the founders of humanistic psychology. He is best known for developing a theory of human motivation. This is commonly referred to as Maslow's Hierarchy of Needs. Now, why do we need to consider this hierarchy of needs?

As parents we are primary caregivers. The first in our children's lives to fulfil their needs. We want to develop within our children what in the psychotherapy world is known as a 'healthy internal working model'. According to Bowlby, who derived this concept, the primary caregiver (most often the parents) generates a template for future relationships through this internal working model. The model has three main features: (1) a model of others as being trustworthy, (2) a model of the self as valuable, and (3) a model of the self as effective when interacting with others.

"If a child is to keep his inborn sense of wonder, he needs the companionship of at least one adult who can share it, rediscovering with him the joy, excitement and mystery of the world we live in." - Rachel Carson

By providing children with the companionship Rachel refers to, we fulfil two tiers of the hierarchy of needs: we provide a sense of safety with which we empower our children with the courage to explore, and we give them a sense of belonging upon which their esteem can be built. It is easy to see that the hierarchy of needs corresponds to the development of the healthy internal working model. If we as the primary caregivers are trustworthy then we generate, *bi'idhnillah* (with the permission of Allah), within our children feature one (internal working model) of others being trustworthy. Through a sense of safety and belonging along with our valuing our children, they will *in sha Allah* establish within them feature two. Once these are present, children are likely to have a self worth with which they can move through the world hence achieving feature three. This will then, by Allah's divine plan and will, allow them to self actualise and fulfil their God-given potential of becoming the awesome individuals they were meant to be.

Why Are Boundaries Important?

According to the Encarta dictionary a boundary is "The official line that divides one area of land from another or the point at which something ends or beyond which it becomes something else or the outer limit of the playing area of a cricket pitch." Healthy relationships have boundaries. This allows us to have a comfortable interdependence with others and enables us to have useful interactions and a confident self-regard. Basically, boundaries create within us the healthy internal working model discussed earlier. Failing to have boundaries generates what Brené Brown describes eloquently: "When we fail to set boundaries and hold people accountable, we feel used and mistreated. This is why we sometimes attack who they are, which is far more hurtful than addressing a behavior or a choice."

Consider the times when children just do as they wish, creating complete havoc whilst you say nothing. You continue in your 'martyresque' stance of doing everything for them and everyone. And eventually when you snap… not a pretty picture. This is why we need to take heed of the following:

"If your boundary training consists only of words, you are wasting your breath. But if you 'do'

boundaries with your kids, they internalise the experiences, remember them, digest them, and make them part of how they see reality." - Henry Cloud

We provide the information by which our children are likely to live their lives by our actions and behaviours. Children do not do as we say. They do as we do. It is proven throughout the animal world: offspring learn through mimicry.

Boundaries also enable:
- Communication
- Protection/Conservation
- Ownership/Responsibility
- Information/Knowledge
- Limits/Structure
- Exclusivity
- Safety/Security
- Constraints

Love and Compassion: The Cornerstone of Relationships

"A loving relationship is one in which the loved one is free to be himself - to laugh with me, but never at me; to cry with me, but never because of me; to love life, to love himself, to love being loved. Such a relationship is based upon freedom and can never grow in a jealous heart." - Leo F. Buscaglia

My understanding of the Prophet (SAW) is that he took people as he found them. He related to them as human beings, whoever they were. We however tend to relate to people as how they 'should' be. Say "a person" is our spouse. Cue a long list of expectations of them. Another is our child. Similar list. What person wouldn't fall short against such walls? We need to be able to accept everyone, including our children, as individuals. They have their own path to tread and their own potential to fulfil.

"Rahma", loving compassion or more commonly mercy, this is an attribute of Allah. The one He (SWT) seems to iterate the most. The Prophet was merciful as well as a mercy to the worlds. It is there as the gel between spouses:
"And amongst His signs is this, that He created mates for you from yourselves that you may find rest in them, and He put between you love and compassion. Surely there are signs in this for a people who reflect." - Quran, Ar-Rum: 21

Love and compassion is mentioned in the context of various relationships. Thus it is a pivotal ingredient to any relationship. And as the following hadith conveys:
Aa'isha (RA) said that a Bedouin man came to the Prophet (SAW) and said "You (people) kiss the children and we do not kiss them." So the Prophet said, **"Is there anything that I can do once Allah has removed mercy from your heart?"** - Bukhari

So the recipe for healthy happy relationships must contain:
- Love
- Compassion
- Time

- Patience
- Affection
- Boundaries
- Individuals
- Space
- Fun
- Acceptance
- Tolerance
- Etc

However, the basis needs to be love and compassion. In the words of Rumi:
"Raise your words, not voice. It is rain that grows flowers, not thunder."

We cannot expect to have relationships with our children when they are teenagers and adults if we have not spent time with them relationally as young children, building bonds and boundaries. The pillars that support our relationships with them need to be established whilst they are young, pre-birth even. As the *athar* of Umar Ibn Al-Khattab (RA) implies we cannot expect our rights if we have not given them theirs. Similarly if we have not gotten to know them as individuals whilst young how can we expect them to trust or even respect us enough to confide in us as they grow? If your children can share with you the small things as they mature then bi'idhnillah they will be able to share with you the big things.

To conclude: *"Stop trying to perfect your child, but keep trying to perfect your relationship with him."* - Dr. Henker

Home to School and Back Again

By Karrie Chariton

I pulled my first child out of school after the completion of first grade, and then again after fourth grade. I pulled my second child out of school after the completion of first grade, and my third child has never been to a traditional brick and mortar school.

My eldest daughter first attended a very small, Islamic preschool and kindergarten in Illinois, USA. There was only a total of 40-50 students in all three classes of the school. Every child knew each other and so did the parents. The school was held in a small house/mosque run by some very motherly Pakistani ladies. Because they had only two official classrooms, classes were also held in the mosque area. It was a great place to learn about Islam and Arabic, mosque etiquettes, and prayers, in addition to learning the letters, numbers, and colors. Allah (SWT) was the focus the whole time. It was a perfect environment at such a young age to instill Islamic values. Masha Allah.

Once our eldest was old enough to go to first grade, we had to transfer her to a larger Islamic school in another area. Although my daughter and I loved the first-grade teacher and she really thrived in school, the school was not what I expected. They had state rules and testing standards to follow. It was basically a public school, but with Muslim children, prayer breaks, and Arabic and Islamic Studies classes. The social problems of a public school still existed, such as cliques, bullying, smoking, etc. Not to mention the tuition cost of the private school was $500 per month. It just didn't have the same environment as the preschool. It was too big and was run as a business. I really liked the personal attention and Islamic environment that the preschool had provided. That is what I wanted to provide my child with, and in the end, I brought her home to achieve just that.

The second time we enrolled our children in school was after we moved to Karachi, Pakistan. Initially, I was homeschooling the two older children. We would take them to parks, but they were shy and uneasy about meeting other children because our children spoke only English and did not understand Urdu. One reason we moved to Pakistan was to have them learn the culture and language, and they were not going to get that sitting indoors with their American mother. So we forced interaction upon them by enrolling them in school. That choice quickly backfired for my middle child. My son struggled in kindergarten where children started school with various levels of English although it was an English medium school. He had a hard time finding his place with some of the other boys who spoke better English than the others. Also, the boys were, frankly, not well behaved and he didn't like that at all. He would cry and cling to me when I dropped him off. It brought tears to my eyes. Although the principal would call and say he was fine ten minutes later, I didn't like the negative impact school was having on him. We hired an Urdu teacher for all of our children to help them with faster language acquisition, but it made for a very long day and little time to play.

Homeschooling is not very common in Pakistan yet, but it is catching on. The families I met mostly homeschooled for religious reasons or the lack of quality education available in all areas of Pakistan. A lot of families had their children in a madrassa for hifz training and then supplemented math and English at home. Some kids would be enrolled back into school after they completed hifz training, but others would continue homeschooling. There was a lack of "Islamic" schools in Karachi. I had expected the schools to integrate Islam into the schools like the Islamic school my daughter attended in the US, but I only found three such schools and some small start-ups before we left Pakistan. There are two schooling tracks in Pakistan, one is the local school system, and the other is the British IGCSE Cambridge system. Most middle and upper-class families in Pakistan choose the Cambridge system since it is more established, viewed as more superior, and serves as preparation for children who are able to study abroad. This Cambridge system is advantageous to the homeschooled children in Pakistan since it is not necessary to go to school to be able to take the final exams for the classes. A child can buy the appropriate books and study it themselves, register to take the final test as an independent, and be able to get the grades they need to then apply for college if they choose. Although most children do attend regular school and then take the tests, Pakistan also has a culture of tuition centers that help students study to pass these GCSE tests. I tend to see this need as a failure to teach the love of a subject. Most students at the school or tuition center are taught only to pass the test. They are not taught Chemistry, for the love of learning Chemistry, as an example. My two oldest children were enrolled in a British school while in Karachi, and I thought it was a very similar curriculum to the US so it didn't really matter what type of school they were in while still young. My only concern as they got older, was would they continue with the British curriculum or would we still stick with the US high school curriculum?

I met a lot of mothers with young kids through the Karachi homeschool group who were not necessarily going to homeschool yet as they were still discovering their paths but were bucking the trend of keeping their kids home instead of enrolling them at a preschool by 18 months or 2 years old. Schooling in Pakistan is a big money making business. The prestigious schools with the good name and reputation basically force you to put your child into school at a young age as a seat filler and money maker until they really need to go to school. There is a waiting list a mile long to get children into these schools. The schools interview these young children so parents spend lots of money on tuition centers to prep their kids for the interview, forcing kids to learn things earlier than necessary. So besides the prestige of sending your child to a brand name school, another reason parents send their children to school at a young age is to be in an English-speaking environment. This is especially important for parents or mothers who don't speak very good English. They see it as advantageous to speak English at a young age. My children did not need to be in school to learn English, I wanted them to learn Urdu.

My youngest was still at home at three years old. It was because of this school system that I received many looks from people in Pakistan who thought I was ridiculous for not putting her into school. Eventually, after a year and a half of the two oldest children going to school, we had to make a decision. Should we enroll our youngest into school for kindergarten or take them all out? After factoring in the safety issues and the quality of the education that was available, we decided to take them out of school again.

After bringing them all back home, it was a relief for me to have them in an emotionally safe place. We hired an Arabic and Urdu teacher to come to the house. We joined a homeschool group, where they made friends and joined in activities. They enjoyed the shorter school days that allowed them lots of time to play with their chickens and ducks. A benefit of homeschooling is that we can provide continuity and it can be done anywhere. We decided to leave Karachi, Pakistan and move to Dubai, U.A.E. After researching the homeschool laws in U.A.E. which allowed expatriates to homeschool, but not the local Emiratis, we continued where we left off. As a family, we were excited to learn about a new place and Arab culture together.

Once we arrived in Dubai, U.A.E. and got our books unpacked, the schooling continued. This time, the school was at our kitchen table rather than the dedicated school room we had in our Karachi home. We had to be responsible to clean up and put books away when we were finished rather than leaving them to lie around. It also brought all three kids to the same table. They were young and still learning to take turns and be patient. There is only one of me and three of them, so I can't help them all at once. They all liked the personal attention, but my eldest who is now finishing 8th grade had become pretty independent in doing her work.

Dubai has a very active and diverse homeschool group. There are kids of all ages and from all over the world. It wasn't until we arrived in Dubai that I realized that I really missed the diversity of cultures we had in the US. In our villa compound after the other school kids arrived home, they all gathered outside to play soccer, ride bikes, and go swimming. My children made friends with kids from Germany, Egypt, Sri Lanka, Canada, Malaysia, and Australia. It was a fantastic opportunity that opened up many discussions on different cultures and values. Since Dubai had much more variety in activities, the kids learned to ice skate, visited old forts, attended book clubs, and learned about Arab culture. Also, since there were so many kids, there were kids of all ages and from all over, it was great to see them all get along, both Muslim and non-Muslim. My eldest daughter had made friends with many girls her age and also attended an Arabic memorization class while in Dubai. I met with moms from all over the world and learned the different ways that families homeschooled their children. It was in Dubai that I learned about umbrella schools from some other American moms. An umbrella school allows you to homeschool or follow their curriculum and receive transcripts and grades for the classes they took. I thought this was especially important for us as a family since I knew most likely our kids would be attending college in the US. Transcripts would be one less hurdle to jump through as a homeschooled high schooler wanting to attend university.

After being in Dubai for a year, we decided to move back to the U.S.A. There was no question that we were going to continue homeschooling. The kids liked being homeschooled. My eldest would like to go to school, but only for the social aspect of making friends which is exactly why we don't want her in school since she will be in high school this fall. There are too many dangers of public school that we would like to avoid as Muslims. My son has been forever traumatized, it seems, from his stint in school. He never wants to go back to traditional school. My youngest, who has never been to school, says she would like to stay home so she has more time to play.

The kids sometimes hear the bus go down our street at 7:30 - 8:00 am and then again at 3:00 pm. Rarely are they awake yet or if they are, they are still in their pajamas, and by 3:00 pm, they are already done and playing outside. I enjoy the relaxed pace of our morning and school routine, not having to rush here and there. Homeschooled children will most likely have some gaps in their education at some time, but they fill those gaps with the time to learn things they want to learn. My son loves playing with his remote control cars, taking them apart, and repairing them. My eldest daughter enjoys playing basketball and writing in her journal and my youngest daughter enjoys playing Minecraft and with remote control cars with her brother. I love that my children have a close bond, we can instill in them our values, and protect them from the unwanted outside influences as long as possible. Having traveled in three countries, I can see that learning truly happens anywhere and anytime. *In sha Allah.*

An Unexpected Journey to Homeschooling My Children

By Omaira Alam

"Education is teaching our children to desire the right things." - Plato

Sometimes I look back on this journey called homeschooling and wonder what have I gotten myself into. Some days are very easy and other days are just so difficult, it would be easier to just give up. I am always wondering about the place of learning in our home. I am always observing my son and daughter - watching what interests them, how they move, what they might need, what might they want to do.

I wonder about how a woman with a Masters in Education, passionate about teaching and learning, married a man who dropped out of high school yet loves reading, and meshed together to find a place where authentic learning can happen for their children.

For me, this journey of homeschooling began almost twenty years ago when I first heard Mr John Taylor Gatto speak about it in Toronto, Canada. He was joined by Shaykh Hamza Yusuf Hanson at the Beyond Schooling conference at the University of Toronto. I was in my last few months of my Bachelor of Education and was caught completely off-guard.

It began a fire in my heart. That was the beginning of the passion that would one day lead me to homeschool my own children. But that journey has always been intertwined with my own growth and learning about what education really is - *what does it mean to be truly educated?* I feel like I am always trying to answer that question. When I first met my husband, I told him about this desire to homeschool our children. In his brilliant mind, he recognized how school can fail some as it failed him. He left school not for a lack of intelligence, but for a lack of interest. He was bored and there were more important things to take care of.

I wonder about that. The courage it takes to say no to a system. I am born of immigrant parents who came first to England, moving later to Scotland and then Canada in pursuit of a better education. When I told them about our decision to homeschool our son - their only grandson

- they balked at the idea. I think a part of them was angry: We left Pakistan so you would have better educational opportunities, and yet here you are saying no to what we left our families behind for…

To them it was always about making a better life for their children. And the only way to do that was through a good education. Funny thing is, at that point they didn't see that we wanted the same thing for our children. We just took a different path than the one that is usually laid out: grade school followed by university, and possibly grad school, if not med school. Robert Frost's oft-quoted words echo in my mind as a sort of mantra to help me keep going:

> "Two roads diverged in a wood, and I -
> I took the one less traveled by,
> And that has made all the difference."
> - Robert Frost

I want my son and daughter to want different things than what I thought was important growing up. I want them to desire reflection, solitude, good company, nature, and genuineness. I want them to desire their Lord and His Beloved and develop an intimate relationship with the Quran, and everything that comes with that. I want them to serve the community through their skills and talents. I want them to really consider the choices they make in life and not just make decisions based upon what everyone expects.

I think that is why my husband and I mesh so well. He took a drastically different path and then became Muslim while serving in the US Navy. Sometimes, I feel that homeschooling is defined in our home by simply doing the unconventional.

There are so many layers to this journey called homeschooling. Each piece uncovers something latent, waiting to emerge. Each period of growth rocks things a little bit so that when you think it will be a mundane journey or you fall into a routine, you are startled awake and you have to continuously remember why you are taking these steps. To me, homeschooling is doing something out of the ordinary, yet so natural for our children. I think that's the clincher: homeschooling acknowledges and celebrates the natural state of our children. Every moment of this unexpected journey reveals this truth.

A Mother's Lap is a Child's First School

By Zawjah Ali

The moment we know we are expecting, we start to make plans for the baby to be. From his clothing to toys, and from his schooling to profession. We think about it all. I was naïve to the term "homeschooling" during my pregnancy and so I did not plan to homeschool. I thought of not being competitive enough and was scared of wasting his precious early years when a child is like a sponge, absorbing and learning a lot. For me, homeschooling is what every mother does, to educate her offspring about every walk of life.

My husband and I decided to enroll our son for *hifdh* and until that time I thought that we would learn together at home. He is now 3.5 years old and I am thankful to Allah that unknowingly we did what is in our best interests. There is a lot of ongoing debate on whether to homeschool or not, listing the merits and drawbacks of both. I am not going to argue any of them but would rather share my own personal journey, how and what we have learned so far. In Pakistan, there is a great trend of enrolling toddlers in 'playgroups'. School now serves as a status symbol, a token of pride to walk boastfully on earth and show off to your relatives. For homeschooling, there is neither strict criteria nor any hard and fast rule to accomplish any specific goal in a targeted time. However, some things aid both learning and understanding.

The S-R connection

We often underestimate the power of stimuli and response, hence offering limited things and ideas to our young children. However, the more an infant is exposed to a variety of things, the more he is receptive of it and more. This might not show up then and there but it will surely unfold in coming months. Despite being ridiculed, I introduced board books to my infant and would point at the pictures and name items aloud along with Urdu and Arabic translations.

We would also name the things we saw outside on our road trips. And yes, using three different languages for the same objects, like when we see a tree, we will say: "tree, shajar, durukht". After a while my son was able to point it out when I asked where the tree was. On accomplishing this I further added some of the characteristics related to objects like that tree is big (kabeer) and the other one is small (sagheer). And he achieved learning these, too.

Natural learning

It is not necessary to make your child sit on a chair at a table at specific timings with a pile of books and then make it a tiring experience of learning. Learning is better absorbed and welcomed when it is done in natural settings. Kids are smart enough to understand cause and effect relationships. They can easily figure things out. An eleven-month-old knows that you will run after him when he goes near to sockets after prior warnings, yet he will smile and go anyway, maybe even wait for your presence. The best approach is to make use of their eagerness to learn whenever they are more receptive, like after they've had their nap or any favorite meal, etc.

Talk to them
For preschoolers talking is a must! The more you tell them the process of things the more their vocabulary will be enriched. For instance, I always used to tell my son that sunlight is good, and that it provides us with vitamin D. Once I asked him to come inside as it was scorching hot in the sun, and he responded, "Utmaa, sunlight is good. It gives us vitamins." I was amazed, alhamdulillah. He accompanies me in the kitchen too, where I say aloud that now I am going to make this curry and will add this and that. He masha Allah knows the cake's ingredients and has learned counting, all just by watching and discussing while we add ingredients together.

Supplicate often
We often make poor or uninformed choices and use wrong approaches, but then we are humans, full of errors. Thus we need the aid of Allah the supreme to guide to our actions and choices, to make it easier on us. It is ok to make mistakes. Mistakes give us room to grow and excel. Trust yourself and be proud of the efforts you are putting in as a mother (or father).

Make a goal
When an aim is set, it is likely to be followed. My ultimate reason to keep my son at home was to fill his heart with love of the mercy of our Lord and His messengers and books.

Attach their heart to Quran
My aim was not just to provide my son with preschool knowledge, but to instill the love for the deen. For that, I read him the Quran, telling him that it has stories in it and that he can read one on his own one day in sha Allah. I narrated him stories of prophets, the miracles and wonder of Allah, and so on. He now knows a lot of stories, alhamdulillah. When my husband and I recite Quran in front of my son and one year old girl, they mimic our actions and feel the same love for the book of Allah. On Fridays we do Surah Al-Kahf pictorial activities, such as cutting triangles to make paper boats and punching it from one side to make a hole to demonstrate the story of Musa and Khidr.

Toys
I provided my son with a small army of men and we named them after the ten blessed companions. We talked about how Abdur Rehman was known for his generosity, Az Zubair Ibn Awwam for bravery, and Sa'd Ibn Abi Waqas for his productivity. We also talked about the battle of Badr and how angels came down to help the Muslims. We put horses along with them and talked about how many were among the armed Quraish, yet they failed. With tangible toys, understanding is high, and remembrance is a surety.

Crafts
Creativity is the essence of everything. We are creations. Creating can bring the best out of every single being. With the help of chart papers, paints, colors, wall hangings, beads, and buttons learning becomes fun. For instance, when my son painted a big fish and then glued

an eye to it, I wrote the dua of Yunus on it and we talked about the story of his impatience and then Allah's power and mercy.

It's not just about weighing the pros and cons to homeschool or not to. When you become a mother, educating a child is the prime and most important responsibility you owe. Trust your motherly capabilities. You just need to unwrap and let the magic begin.

Deschooling 101

By Zakiya Mohamed

What is Deschooling?

Deschooling is a process whereby students and parents detach themselves from the learning mind-set of the formal schooling system, by taking a complete break from school routines, designated subjects and grades, and standardised testing. This is sometimes done for a transitional period to unwind and re-orientate themselves from that system into one of the types of home-schooling or permanently as a way of schooling itself, called unschooling.

Why is it done?

Home-schooling can take so many forms, and deschooling can allow you as a parent to discover which, if any, will suit your children's learning styles, through observation during this 'free' time. This can avoid the confusion and possible frustration often experienced when a parent simply leaps straight from formal schooling into doing the same type of learning at home.

Simply allowing children to get back into exploring the world (even if just for a while), and observing them do so, can reveal our children's natural talents, and how they can best learn.

In his TED video titled *Do Schools Kill Creativity?* Ken Robinson tells of how Gillian Lynne went from a child referred to a therapist for not being able to concentrate, to the founder of the Gillian Lynne Dance School, choreographer of world-class theatre productions such as CATS, and a multi-millionaire. All of this came about because that therapist didn't put Lynne's fidgety behaviour down to ADHD, but rather recognised her bodily-kinaesthetic learning style and recommended dance school instead.

Once we let go of the need to cling to the 'norm' of mass schooling, and the anxiety that our kids aren't doing enough fast enough, we can allow ourselves and our children to decompress, and begin consciously seeking out the best ways to go about home education.

Unconscious process

The curious thing about deschooling is that a lot of the time, parents don't consciously seek to do it, but rather end up in the position by accident, because their initial attempt at getting right into home-schooling has seemingly failed, or not worked out the way they expected it to, or simply because they want to give themselves and their children a break.

Editor of the *Fitra Journal*, Brooke Benoit tells of how she began home-schooling her son with a traditional curriculum approach - which didn't succeed - and then found herself taking a step back and deschooling unconsciously:
"Sometime later I would come across the term "deschooling" on blogs and websites, and that's when I realized that was what I did. I deschooled myself by taking a break from replicating the

institutionalized form of education (I was essentially trying to recreate a school-like institution in my home) and learning about the education process - how children can and do learn. It was a completely different experience once I deschooled myself."

Did she say deschool *herself*?
Yes!

The reason that most parents take their kids out of the formal, institutionalised schooling system is because they are dissatisfied with some or all of the system, and want to offer their kids something better at home. But when parents have grown up through that very system, their minds still hold onto some of the ideas that traditional schooling propagates. So even though we may realise the need for change and start taking steps in that direction, we can easily fall back into simply re-creating a similar system at home.

This is often the biggest challenge for home-schooling parents - moving away from simply bringing the school environment (in a smaller form) into their homes. According to author and unschooling advocate Sandra Dodd: "Parents need to dismantle the framework on which they're hanging what they think they know about learning." It may be necessary and is certainly helpful for parents who have been traditionally schooled themselves, to deschool in order to free their subconscious minds from turning toward the same old routines and ways of learning and teaching found in schools.

Unschooling mom and author for *The Natural Child Project*, Jan Hunt believes that when we break free from the ways our minds have been conditioned to learn, "we can re-discover the natural love of learning we were born with".

The general guideline period for deschooling is one month for every year of formal schooling attended, even (some say *especially*) for parents.

How exactly is it done?
There is no one single, right way to deschool. (It's about breaking the rules, after all!)
But there are some things you can do to develop an interesting and fun culture of learning:

1. Visit museums, exhibitions, art galleries, or play parks.
2. Play games with the kids or let them play with siblings, or other home-schoolers.
3. Use the deschooling time to feel yourself letting go and unwinding, and to explore the different options for homeschooling.
4. Read together, and model your own interest in various reading material for your kids to follow suit.
5. Involve the kids in cooking meals, and shopping for groceries. Let them feel involved, responsible, and more independent as individuals.
6. Allow them to take up crafts, DIY projects, or a sport. Give them choices, allow them to try things, and change as they feel like for a while.
7. Let them be free to look up things in the library, on the internet, and on TV (monitoring age-appropriate content of course).
8. Allow them to get involved in community projects or volunteer at the local mosque.

Let children's interests channel them through these and other activities, as they get the hang of pursuing learning about certain things, and leaving out others. Be the facilitator for their self-led learning, rather than their teacher.

Importantly, especially for older children - explain to them why they are leaving formal schooling, and that this process is to decompress, and try out different ways of learning, for them to enjoy and thrive.

But don't get into the theory of anti-institutionalised learning, or how you want to revolutionise their learning via deschooling with your kids. It must be a transition into learning that feels more natural, and not like another task or experiment they are being forced into.
It is a time to relax, and rediscover natural curiosity, personal passions, and interests.

De-schooling can lead to unschooling
Parents may come to realise over a period of deschooling that letting go of routine, learning in time-blocks per subject, and fixed curricula is actually working better for their children. They may notice increased motivation for learning with time. If they decide to continue with this unstructured, child-led way of learning, they can move from deschooling for a time, to unschooling as a complete way of learning.

But is it for everyone?
If you are the type of parent who prefers structure and a smaller school-like set-up at home, you may know exactly what you would like to achieve in your home-schooling environment, and just get straight into that.

I have seen this example in one of the home-schooling families I work with. Teen homeschoolers Ayaaz, Imaan, and Kaamil Kalla shifted from traditional schooling to a smaller curriculum, with a greater focus on Qur'an memorisation, and designated time-blocks for 'secular' tuition. They learn certain subjects of interest to them, which are recognised as credits at local South African universities. Having left formal schooling at the end of a school year, they began home-schooling immediately at the beginning of the following year. Though they had choose home-schooling over going back to school any day, they enjoy the structure of their current learning programme, and feel that some structure is necessary to keep them on track, as do their parents. What they like most about their home-schooling is their one-on-one experience with tutors. Because their school day has been shortened, they get plenty of time to pursue other interests such as building crafts and playing video games.

Each household, and every child is different. As for the constricting effects of large scale, institutionalised learning on children's minds, there is certainly a growing worldwide consciousness of it. Deschooling may give us the time we need to explore the alternatives.
Discover more on these sites:
http://unschoolingsupport.com/deschooling/
http://sandradodd.com/deschooling/
http://a2zhomeschooling.com/beginning_home_school/deschooling_recovering_from_school/

Chapter 2
HOMESCHOOLING IN THE DIGITAL AGE

Are You a Digital Immigrant or Digital Native?

By Sumaia b. Michel

Do you know what a VCR is? Clearly, you are a digital immigrant. You are a stranger, learning the ways of the strange (virtual) land you have landed in. Welcome to the Digital Age. Let's face it, many of our children are better at handling technologies than we are. Do you understand what they are talking about when they are sharing their latest conquest on their PS4 with their friends? They have been born and raised with the digital language. They consider an age without cell phones ancient, and they cannot imagine how you survived without Facebook. As a parent, you do not fluently speak the language of these digital natives. That doesn't mean you are digitally inept, but the 'digispeak' doesn't come as easy to us as it does to our children.

This digital (generation) gap is hard for parents in general, but can be even more challenging for homeschoolers. After all, we have chosen to be solely responsible for our children's education, haven't we? (What were we thinking?!) So now it is up to us to decide how much digital influence we allow in our households.

As with so many things, there are advantages and disadvantages. For one, we decide how much our digital natives immerse into the virtual world. Secondly, we avoid the peer pressure of owning the latest models and games, which can surely benefit our wallet. On the other hand, it is far easier to have a school policy restricting the use of cellphones and pads than you trying to convince your children why these devices are not allowed during 'school time'. Or, why they have limited screen time and have other activities that they have to do. (I don't know about you, but I am having a hard time convincing my seven year old he cannot play Minecraft every waking hour.)

And then, unexpectedly, I am having a fantastic conversation with my ten year old explaining to me why she does not like to play with certain friends, because they spend all their time on their screens and little time actually playing, or having a good talk. In these moments, I know why I chose to homeschool. I know that, despite the digital gap, I can connect with my digital native and offer her a balanced view of the (virtual) world.

Technology: Necessary and Not so Bad at All

By Sumaia b. Michel

Digital technologies have rapidly changed a variety of things in our lives: communications are lightning fast, social relationships take place in the virtual world, and all sorts of gadgets have (supposedly) increased our well-being. Similarly, technology is having consequences for education, both for schools as well as for homeschoolers. As homeschoolers, we have a myriad of options to choose from as to how, when and what technology we wish to implement in our homeschool curriculum. In this article I will give a brief overview of how digital technology[1] could be used in our pursuit to educate our children. For the purposes of this article, we will not discuss digital technologies as a form of recreation.

Despite the fact that many of us already make use of some or many digital technologies, parents are often divided on the topic. Some fear technologies, while other parents laud technologies as the new 21st century method of homeschooling. There are both clear advantages and disadvantages of digital technologies for homeschoolers.

Proponents of the use of technologies often focus on the increase in skills the use of technologies can bring their children. Children can be more engaged in the topic, work better independently, learn scheduling and are able to create digital products such as videos, audios or podcasts. All of these skills are essential to learn.

Those that fear the negative consequences of digital technologies point out the social disengagement children display when they are engrossed in digital activities. Another concern is the loss of particular academic skills, such as handwriting and dictionary skills. Loss of social skills and virtual interaction is a major worry for many homeschooling parents. Often, students find it more difficult to read large amounts of text on a digital screen than from paper. Additionally, many parents feel children will not consider other forms of entertainment or resources.

In reality, it isn't about whether technology is bad or good, it's about how technology is being used. Clearly, each argument mentioned above has a point. Homeschooling often follows several phases, even though they usually happen simultaneously and repeatedly. These phases are the preparation phase, the teaching phase, the enrichment or skills enhancement phase, and the 'after-school' phase. Whether you are a novice or a veteran homeschooler, or just merely considering homeschooling, I have outlined the use of technology in these different phases of homeschooling below.

Preparation Phase
In the preparation phase, many of us rely on technology in a myriad of ways. We educate ourselves on homeschooling, research curricula and schools, read up on the feedback or experiences of others, and compare prices. And let's not forget the many hours of shopping for books and materials we save ourselves by simply ordering online! A computer with internet access has given us immediate access to plenty of resources we can use.

Teaching Phase
When we have decided on a curriculum or a school and selected our materials, technology can also play a role in the actual teaching phase. There are online schools, which include online access to teachers, counselors and even all books. Parents can choose between a part time and a full time course load online. Another form of online teaching could be a tutor or an elective class. Digital technologies also offer different sources of knowledge for different learning styles. Auditory or visual learners will enjoy content in multimedia format. Students with learning challenges such as dyslexia could benefit by reading from a specialized screen instead of pages. In all these cases, internet access plays a substantial role in homeschooling.

Enrichment Activities or Skills Enhancement Phase
For enrichment activities or skills enhancement, technology can also be of great assistance. Technology could be a tool to teach independent learning when doing a project or when taking a student-led approach, as in unschooling or research-based learning. Technology offers multimedia options such as audio and video integration. Children with a specific interest have the possibility to find a network of like-minded people and loads of resources.

'After-school' Phase
For 'after-school' activities, outdoor fun or clubs to attend, technology often works as the village drum: new clubs, activities, and meetings with other homeschool families are all announced through Facebook, WhatsApp groups, Twitter, etc. And for some moral support when the going gets tough, finding encouragement through similar networks is, for many parents, a much needed service.

For those homeschooling in regions without plentiful paper-based text resources, digital content can have an added value. For these families, it can solve several logistic problems, such as the higher expenses of shipping, restricted access to libraries and less alternative resources for hands-on learning (for example farms, workplace visits and more).

How parents wish to use technology in their homeschooling is, after all, up to them. As with many choices homeschooling parents are faced with, common sense is often the best guidance. But where to start? It is wise to first decide what you wish to teach your children and why. Once that is sorted out, see where technology can be included. In the end, children will have to be able to master several 21st century skills, including digital technologies. However, technology should be a means to an end and not the end itself.

[1] Included in digital technologies is every device or material used to solve practical problems encountered in homeschooling that make use of computers or the internet.

Guiding Our Children on the Internet

By Shaykh Ismail Kamdar

Many of us choose to homeschool our children as a means of protecting them from the harmful elements of society, and from bad company. Yet in the back of our minds there remains a worry: *What about the bad elements of society and bad company they can access online?*

Dealing with the internet and its usage is a difficult topic for many Muslims parents. On one hand, the internet is full of amazing learning websites, documentaries, educational YouTube videos, and Islamic websites, and is also a great way to stay in contact with family and friends. But then there is the dark side that all parents are aware of. There are the pornographic websites, the cyberbullying, the extremist websites that entice young Muslims to violence, and many other things that parents wish didn't exist. But they do, and we need to be practical in finding a solution to dealing with it.

Knowing about the dark net has raised great concern from parents. Do we allow our children to use the internet? At what age do we allow it? How do we restrict their access to unfavourable websites? What do we do if we catch a teenager on an immoral website? I hope to answer in this article these and many more dilemmas.

The Islamic Ruling on the Internet

Before we begin, it is important to understand the Islamic ruling on using the internet. The internet is a tool, and like all other tools, the ruling is based on its usage and not the tool itself. If the internet is used for halal and beneficial purposes, it is permissible. In fact, using the internet can even be ibaadah when used as a means of dawah and spreading Islamic knowledge.

However, when the internet is misused to commit any type of sin, then its usage becomes a sin for that moment only. To make a mass ruling that people should not use the internet at all goes against primary principles of Fiqh which include, "The original rule of a thing is permissibility" and that "The religion is practical." Therefore, we can conclude that using the internet is permissible, and it is only prohibited when it is being used for unIslamic reasons.

Now that we understand the ruling on using the internet, here are a few practical steps for helping your children learn to use it responsibly:

1. Teach them to be responsible in every aspect of their lives

Responsibility is not just related to the internet. As Muslim parents, it is our duty to teach our children to be responsible. We can do this by teaching them about the Afterlife and accountability for their deeds. We can also do this by giving them responsibilities from a young age, instead of spoiling them. A responsible character should be part of who they are, in person as well as online, and is the first step to responsible usage of the internet.

2. Discuss with them openly the dangers of the internet
Parents need to be transparent with their children about the dangers of anything. Of course, conversations need to be kept age appropriate. But children need to know that bad things exist on the internet, just like anywhere else, and they need to know about the many ways in which these websites can harm them. An informed child is less likely to fall into any online traps, especially if they are aware of why something is bad and the harm it can cause to them.

3. Have clear rules, policies, expectations and repercussions
Communication is key to discipline. If you want your children to follow your rules, then these rules need to be very clear. Parents must set age-appropriate rules and policies for internet usage. Such rules could include limiting internet time and data consumption, and allowing parents to occasionally check their devices to monitor usage.

Expectations also need to be very clear. Let your child know that you are trusting him/her with the internet and expect them to use it only for permissible things. Likewise, the repercussions of not meeting expectations and violating the rules should be clear and upheld.

Some suggested repercussions include confiscation of devices, suspension of internet privileges, or limiting internet usage to study purposes only.

4. For younger children, keep internet devices in the open
Children who are under the age of twelve do not need their own mobile devices or internet devices in their bedrooms. For older children, it can be debated either way. Younger children should be given access to the internet via family computers which are kept in a place where parents can monitor their usage.

This could mean having the computer set up in the lounge, study, or kitchen, but not in the child's private bedroom. This will help keep them from straying to incorrect websites.

With older kids, parents need to have serious conversations with each other about when it would be appropriate to give them their own mobile phones or access to private devices. Eventually, as they grow you will need to start trusting them more and letting them go. I will discuss this point in more details in point six.

5. Install software that blocks out immoral websites and ads
There are many tools available online to clock immoral websites and monitor internet usage. If your children use the internet while you are not there to supervise, then you should consider investing in good internet security. Install ad-blockers, pornography blockers and website trackers. Let your children know that these things are installed and that you will be monitoring their usage through these tools.

6. Trust your teenagers and give them some semi-privacy
As your children grow older, you will have to eventually start giving them some space. This

is especially true for teenagers. Teenagers need privacy and space to grow. If they are under constant monitoring, they grow rebellious and difficult to deal with.

In order to have a good relationship with your teenager, you need to give her privacy and respect that space. At the same time, that teenager needs to know that the parent is still in charge and there are consequences for abusing such privileges.

7. Deal with mistakes realistically and leave the channels of communication open
At the end of the day, your children are human and will still make mistakes. Expecting perfection from them is not practical and will lead to them lying to you and living a double life. Be practical in how you deal with your children's mistakes. Do not allow emotion to dictate what you say or do. Remember that your duty is to guide them towards the straight path, not to chase them away.

Teach them the importance of istighfaar and tawbah, show them practical ways to avoid falling into mistakes again, and have honest discussions with them about the temptations they will face at each stage of life and how to cope with them.

These tips will help you maintain a good relationship with them, and also keep their internet usage halal and beneficial.

Raising a Reader Among Viewers

By Asma Ali

Fun Fact: Reading for just six minutes a day reduces stress by 68 percent.

I am particularly fond of this piece of information simply because I have loved reading for as long as I can remember - in fact, my earliest memory is turning the page of a supersized book at nursery school when I'm sure I was supposed to be doing something else. Fast-forward a couple of decades and you will still find me quietly flipping through some writing or another, when I know I should be doing something else. For me, reading remains the quintessential hobby that creates a comforting haven away from the daily grind. As a parent, I have always been quite keen to transfer my own interest and love of books to my children so you can imagine my surprise (and heartbreak!) when my eldest one day exclaimed, "I HATE reading!"

It was completely unexpected. I had followed the classic advice of introducing a variety of literature well before my son could read alone and regularly made time for a bedtime story. Despite this, I knew he would now rather cozy up with the iPad and shoot at aliens than escape with a book, which brings me nicely to another not-so-fun fact: with all the technological advances recent years have brought, reading for pleasure is on the decline amongst kids and teens.

Let's face it, entertainment for children is far snazzier these days thanks to the gaming industry. Competing with apps on the iPad, playing or viewing on the laptop, Xbox, Nintendo... we all have one (or two!) of these gadgets and so the humble paperback is often overlooked.

Why reading still matters

Neil Gaiman, an English author, stated that there is a difference between a reader and someone who can read. I believe that distinction can be made with one who loves literature and derives pleasure from it as opposed to reading out of necessity. So, first and foremost, it is important to think of reading as an enjoyable activity, but that does not mean it is void of practical benefit. Both fiction and non-fiction contribute significantly to a child's academic and social development in the following ways:

Increased vocabulary - Books aid our children in exposing them to new language and vocabulary that is generally more sophisticated than what they will hear in a typical day. An increased word bank allows children to express themselves clearly and communicate with confidence.

Greater writing and speaking ability - Reading is a surefire way to become familiar with grammar, spelling, and writing styles without actually studying, which in turn ensures a good grasp of the English language (or whatever language they are reading in). Again, this aids children to speak articulately and with eloquence.

Enhanced emotional intelligence - Fiction allows a child to see the world from a different perspective. Following a new character or situation strengthens the capacity to identify what someone else is feeling or thinking. Readers are also proven to exhibit higher levels of empathy and compassion!

Boosts creativity - Reading provides a good workout for mental fitness and stimulates the brain. It develops creativity and sparks the imagination as children who begin to visualize what they read, for example they can see the characters and settings being described. Creative thought leads to mental agility and both are essential for cognitive development in children.

You might have found that digital devices have actually made it easier to draw children back into reading, as stories are brought to life with attractive animation, but a recent scientific study has shown that the advantages of reading from an actual book are far greater. These benefits include better focus, concentration and comprehension of what is being read. And that's why I'm making the case to put the Kindles and e-books away and get those books back out!

How to encourage reading for pleasure

DO limit screen time - Pulling children away from electronics is hard and a constant battle, I know firsthand. And I know this may not necessarily mean kids will head straight for the books, but the longer they spend on these gadgets, the less time they have for anything else - including reading. Try setting aside a time or whole day that is device-free so they have time to enjoy something else. They will learn that TV and computers are not the only source of entertainment, nor are they the only place that children can enter a new world. Kids might opt to play outside or lounge, but on occasion they might decide to set up a tent with their blankets and pillows and read!

DON'T nag - Constantly pushing your child to read when they don't want to might just put them off reading altogether so tread carefully. Remember, it's supposed to be a joyful experience and not something forced. If you don't have a set time for reading, suggest it as an activity when you think they will be more receptive to the idea. Praise them when they do pick up a book and read even if it is only for ten minutes.

DO let your child choose what they want to read - It's easy to want to fill the shelves with our childhood favorites, but allowing a child to pick their own book will probably result in them actually finishing it. The more they enjoy it, the more they will do it. They might just surprise you with their choice and reveal a new interest! Provide a varied selection of literature at home and, if you're blessed to have one near you, take regular trips to the library to find age-appropriate books. Suggest titles but let them decide if they want to give it a go or not.

TIP: Older children might like to set themselves a "Reading challenge." There are a number of challenges available to print online where kids choose their own titles to fit a genre or you could design one yourself. The point is to make reading fun.

DON'T discourage reading the same book again and again - This is probably more common with younger readers. It can be tiresome for you if you are reading aloud with them, but kids love familiarity and pointing out the words they know.

DO model reading, read aloud, and escape together - A common mistake is to stop reading aloud to children once they can read independently, but all kids enjoy being read to so continue even when they reach that stage. Not only is this a great bonding opportunity, but it makes the reading experience a lot more exciting! Bear in mind that if a reluctant reader is not exposed to anyone reading at home, it is far more difficult to convey the concept of reading for pleasure. Enthusiasm is contagious - when children see how passionate you are about reading, it slowly begins to instill a love of books in them and will motivate a child to read alone. Take a special 'time out' from routine and introduce reading as an opportunity to escape together.

DON'T turn every book into an assessment - OK. I'm guilty of this one and I'm sure a lot of homeschooling parents in particular are too: Your child's just finished putting down a book and you're ready to pounce on them with a list of questions to test their literacy skills. By all means, show interest in what they're reading but don't turn their recreation into a learning point. Critical reading and scanning texts for information purposes is a skill and reading for pleasure is a great way to practice and develop it. Leave them be.

DO subscribe to a magazine - Yes, magazines are books too and a great additional resource to have. And who doesn't like receiving something in the post? With a diverse range of topics to choose from, such as sports, arts and crafts, science, and even Islam for kids, this is a really fun way for children to read and engage with their own unique interests. Magazines are colorful and jam-packed with information, easy to dip into, and they give the children something to look forward to.

DON'T use reading as an incentive to get back on a device - This is a sticky one. I've had to stop myself from doing this as I realized it made reading come across as a chore and secondary to digital entertainment, rather than a way to unwind and relax. I much prefer when reading is done with no strings attached and because children want to read from their own desire. I recently read some sage advice that the best reward for reading was more books and more time to read them.

DO buy books as presents - Even the most averse reader can't resist the allure of the displays at a bookshop. Go ahead and buy books of their choosing as a treat and encourage your child to buy books as gifts for others to highlight their value and worth. We often buy gadgets and treat them like prized items, do the same with books!

DON'T give up! I sincerely believe all children can acquire a love of reading whether they are simply reluctant or genuinely struggle to read. When my son told me he hated it, I promptly quoted J.K Rowling, "If you don't like to read, you haven't found the right book." And that's all there is to it. Keep trying.

Reading is crucial and an invaluable part of your child's life. It can be used as a source of comfort, a way to relax, and a means to introduce a world of new experiences and imagination. Establishing a love of books and reading for pleasure corresponds with a love of learning and a passion for knowledge. Despite the introduction of high-tech entertainment, there can and should always be room for a good old book.

Creating an IT Study Unit for Screen-free Children

By *Klaudia Khan*

When it comes to the use of digital technology in our home I am a traditionalist: I believe it is better and healthier for children to learn from 'real' rather than virtual. Our homeschooling is based on books and field trips and my children don't own any electronic devices except for two old mobile phones that don't work, but are very useful in pretend play. It's not that technology is completely absent in our home; both mine and my husband's work requires using a computer and we do have smart phones that perhaps sometimes require our attention too often. I know that smart devices and a constant feed of news can be addictive. And this is my primary reason why I would rather keep my children at a safe distance from them.

On the other hand, I am fully aware that IT skills nowadays are as important as literacy and I don't want my children to miss out on learning how to use electronic devices to their advantage. Even though they don't have any allocated screen time - and certainly no time for games - they do get a chance to use the computer when they call family abroad through Skype and occasionally use my husband's work tablet to create simple pictures in Paint. I hope they are getting the message behind the restriction - computers can be useful tools, but they have to be used in moderation.

In my quest to make learning about computers possible without actually spending too much time in front of screens, I came across a handful of printed books and resources that do just that. And because I like our learning materials to be beautiful, (not much workbook-like) and as my children are still very young my two choices are *Hello Ruby: Adventures in Coding* by Linda Liukas and *Dot.* by Randi Zuckerberg.

Hello Ruby is very attractive with its lovely bright pictures and cute characters. It certainly attracts children's attention and doesn't lose it as it engages little readers in the quest to help Ruby find the hidden jewels. The story itself is very simple, but the creative activities for each chapter make it fun. The characters that the girl meets at each stage are sure to become children's favourites. Because the main character is a girl, and because of the illustration style, the book might be more attractive to girls, but then I have only daughters, so I can't really tell. However, IT technology is stereotypically male-dominated, so if there is a book about programming that is directed specifically to girls then all the better.

The book claims to be "the world's most whimsical way to learn about technology, computing and coding." It doesn't give any specific instruction on any software, but rather aims at making the way a computer works a bit more clear and trains in abstract thinking and the language of code. Children can learn how to break big problems into small ones by creating step-by-step plans, they find out what loops and algorithms are, and what it means to debug. I must admit that I have learned some interesting stuff from the book myself!

The activities included in the book vary from playing robot-like games, to matching pairs, and designing board games. They are fun and unusual and sure to spark children's interest. There are also more activities and ideas available on the website at **helloruby.com**.

I like the book for the way it teaches without seeming didactic and because, as the authors say, "There's plenty to learn in programming logic and culture before showing children a single screen" and this is just what I was looking for.

The second book that I chose for our IT studies is *Dot.* by Randi Zuckerberg. *Dot.* is a picture book that again does not teach any computer skills, but rather addresses the issue of the correct approach to IT devices and social media. Dot, the book's character, "knows a lot" the story starts. "She knows how to tap, to swipe, to share…" but then her mother sends her outside to play and she is again happy doing all those things: tapping - as in tap-dancing, swiping - the paint on the canvas, and sharing a biscuit with her dog. Dot understands that virtual life is not all there is to life and it's always fun to go out and play to "recharge, restart and reboot". This is the main message of this lovely illustrated book.

It might seem an odd choice for us, as my children do not own any electronic devices and certainly do not know how to 'share' on Facebook, but I have chosen this book because it can teach the specific media-vocabulary, and at the same time send the message - screen-time is never better than playtime.

* See our Resources section for suggestions of other books about IT for children.

Best Practices for Technology in Home Education:
Interview With Dr. Alan Fortescue

By Brooke Benoit

Alan Fortescue, PhD is the High School Director at Oak Meadow and recently gave a conference presentation called "Impact of Technology on Home Education." I asked Alan to explain some of the key points of the presentation and further elaborate on technology and homeschooling for *Fitra Journal* readers.

Brooke Benoit: You have a four part checklist for using technology as a homeschooler. Will you please explain how parents can use this list?
Alan Fortescue, PhD: First, why we are using it and what is it meant to achieve? In regard to this item parents should think about both a general overall approach to technology and its task specific use.

In general, before parents integrate technology into any learning situation, they should ask themselves if doing so is truly necessary or relevant. So many people today turn on the computer as a starting point or way to determine what should be learned without thinking about why they have done so. Often times this actually prevents the development of cogent learning goals because parents become lost in the unending realm of content without first defining and understanding what one's learning goals are. A quality learning situation, then, starts with defining what it is a student should learn, and, crucially, why they should learn. If you cannot explain to yourself why something is important to learn your child will not learn it. They may be compelled to memorize that information but they will not retain that information over the long-term.

For meaningful learning to occur it is vital that course material/learning goals be applicable to a student's real world existence - this is how information is transferred into knowledge. Once a parent has defined the What and Why of a lesson, they could then proceed to the How of teaching it. In what way does the material need to be positioned, explained, experienced, questioned, and explored, to help the learner understand what it means and its importance? At this point a parent may decide that some form of technology is useful. Which technology is used and why will depend upon the subject matter and purpose of the learning. Art versus social studies versus math, for example. Two examples:

Drawing lesson
Learning goals
- to teach a student how to use different line weights
- to help them see how artwork is constructed
- to help them understand why people make art
- how its construction creates it meaning/expressive value

Items to be used
- different types of pencils, different types of paper, computer

Tech needs/use
- use computer to find master artworks to examine

Detail
- If you are trying to teach a child about the importance of different line weights (which has to do with the width and darkness or lightness of a drawn line and the different density of pencil lead one uses to create such differences) you might first start by exploring some of the reasons we (as humans) create art - to express our emotions, or to express complex concepts that are hard to explain in language. In this exploration, you could find two or three different masterworks through a Google search - doing the search together so the student learns how to do such a search. You might find images like these: *http://goo.gl/ecb4cX* and *https://goo.gl/g53vqu* and then talk with your child about what she sees in these images, how what she sees makes her feel, what she thinks the artist was trying to express, and *why* she thinks the artist was trying to express this. You then might ask your child to closely examine how the images have been drawn. Asking things like: where are the dark areas, where are the light areas, how do they think the artist created these different spaces, and what power do these changes in tonality have in regard to shaping how one feels about the artwork.

Then you might demonstrate a series of simple lines, asking the student to draw the same. This activity creates a physical/tactile sense for the act of drawing lines that is incorporated into the body differently than a purely cognitive explanation. After this exercise, you could set the child free to do her own Google search for drawings that inspire or confound or challenge her, and have her explain to you what she sees in these drawings and what she feels they mean. Ultimately, you might have her choose a particular drawing to do a master study of. In this way, technology is used as a tool with a clear purpose, a purpose that existed because you defined it before you began the lesson with the student, and a purpose that evolves as the child expresses her own understanding of the subject matter and her personal interest. The technology never takes over the learning goals as the focus.

Geography/Social Studies lesson
Learning goals
- to help students understand how local environments and resource usage/scarcity shape geopolitical conflict
- to understand how consumer markets in the US can drive negative impacts internationally

- to understand the long term-social consequences of one's actions
- to think about social responsibility beyond one's borders; to value human health and thriving above consumer capital needs
- to critically examine the logic of a market economy

Items to be used
- example of how the American lumber market (at Home Depot) is responsible for deforestation that led to environmental (and thus social/economic) collapse in Honduras
- peer-reviewed articles, newspaper articles, government reports, film or video exploring the issue
- a local example (in the student's community that helps to act as a simple example of the complex issue they will study - putting it into a more immediate context)

Tech use
- use the computer to research articles and government reports and watch videos on the subject
- find several examples of articles and videos on the issue (some based on actual reliable research and analysis, some inaccurate and biased) before introducing the unit to the student
- As part of the introduction of the unit, do a mini-unit on research in which you explore what constitutes good sources and what are not good sources. Bring up samples and explore together, looking for things like where it is published, who wrote it and their credentials, when it was published, is it based on first hand accounts or second hand, etc.

Final project
- Conclude with a research paper that explains the situation in detail (the players, the issues, the challenges, the destruction, the politics) and a five-minute public service announcement about the issue in which the student will take a position and prepare the video for public consumption.

Secondly, allow children to be involved, but create understanding and boundaries so tech doesn't take over. This has to do with not being too controlling over your child's use of (and experimentation with) technology. It is important to know why you are using it and to set up some ground rules, but at the same time you do not want to shut off a child's curiosity and freedom to explore in ways that may be really important. Think of it like teaching your child how to ride a bike. At first you stay close, steady the bike, and walk along with them, but as they grow in understanding and skill you back off, allowing them freedom to grow on their own. It's a balance.

Third point - discuss potential dangers. Just as we would do with all potentially hazardous things our children become involved with, we need to help them understand the risk and rewards in terms that they can understand. Approach this like a conversation in which you are both learning something rather than a time to scare them or threaten them (things people do not respond well to). I approach this from the sense of, hey, look at all the amazing things we can do with the computer, all it has to offer; but, then wonder out loud about some of the negative aspects of too much screen time. To use the rock climbing metaphor in my presentation - an amazing sport full of challenges that expand who one is and one's ability to problem solve under stress as well as to control one's mind and to find oneself in incredible natural setting - it is also a very dangerous sport the requires my child to understand those dangers. At the same time, it is vital not to drown a passion for something with fear. So, when taking my own children climbing, I talk about what the sport is like first hand: why I love it, how I think about approaching a climb, my relationship with rock (I LOVE rock), the sensory tactile experience of climbing, what it means to me mentally and emotionally. But not all at once; this all unfolds over the period of several hours during a hiking/climbing expedition.

The same thing could be done with using a computer. Model behavior and good use as you introduce children to using computers. Talk about what you are protecting them from; tell them what you might be afraid of for yourself and for them. Tell them why you stop using your computer after a certain amount of time, because of the potential health consequences.

Fourth and last checklist item: moderate and make time for non-tech play. The best way to do this is to model this behavior yourself. Children follow the lead of action more so than words. If you help them leave their desk and go outside with them to hike or play, or talk as you garden, or ride a bike, this will help them not only see that it is okay to get outdoors, but fun and fulfilling.

Brooke: As you have pointed out, the American Academy of Pediatrics has a guideline for screentime and children that is basically 0-2 years old no tech, 2-6 years old 2 hours daily, after 6 years old 4 hours daily. But what kind of screens for which age groups are we talking about? For instance, what age group should have a handheld device versus a PC, and why? What about a laptop?
Alan: I want to update this - the most recent release of AAP states: no screen time of any kind 0-2 years (computers, phones, televisions, etc); 1-2 hours per day for ages 3-18. For further reading see:
• https://goo.gl/2Tp7dN
• https://goo.gl/HbyBqK

Per your question, screen-time is screen time regardless of size or mobility. It's about what happens to the brain while using computers (which phones are). Another resource to check: http://goo.gl/9plWW2

Brooke: Wikispaces - many schools are now assigning students to do wiki projects (usually private), why is this (or similar) an important (or not) activity for homeschoolers to consider participating in?
Alan: I soft pedaled my feelings about tech in the presentation. Truly, there are few useful applications of tech beyond being a research tool (which videos can be a part of that, viewing art, exploring ecosystems, places, architecture, lit etc.). It is humans who must do the work, the thinking, the putting together of ideas and transform that into knowledge. Wikispaces and other software solutions that purport to be the school in many ways are horrible and I think do a great deal of damage to the developing mind. I would eschew them all.

Tech solutions most often are more about sales - and finding catchy ways to capture market share than they are peer reviewed, tested, analyzed, and useful tools for learning. Business people make these things and know little about education. The truth is there is no easy way to educate, it is not something you can or should put in a bottle and make simple for all to use. It is an exciting, dynamic, and often challenging process that is always best done human to human (which can be at a distance too). It is the human who must learn, who must push their mind (which can feel uncomfortable) to understand new concepts/ideas, develop new skills. If the computer does everything for us, what is the point of living? Being alive is about experience, about doing, and feeling, about making meaning, about the sense we have in our heart and soul when we know that we know something.

Brooke: At this point I assume most parents are aware of the health implications of overuse of internet/technology by children, but in case they aren't could you please list the most common ones?
Alan: I think most parents are not truly aware of the health impacts, otherwise I think we would be seeing less of it. Read the resources I included above; here are some more:
http://goo.gl/jAoyoe
http://goo.gl/KDNdUY
http://goo.gl/TalH3n

Brooke: Please explain how this problem of no down time to process information (kids jump from app to app, info to info) means less critical thinking and decision making from children? And how can parents avoid this?
Alan: Above all, critical thinking takes time. One must mull over an idea/thought/action to fully understand it, evaluate different potential outcomes or iterations or possibilities. New ideas and creativity in particular require one to stay with a thought for a long period of time, develop it over days/weeks/even years. Think about how kids use tech: they are jumping from image to image, LMAO, LOL; and program to program; and they're rewarded for more, quicker = better. Research shows significant difference in what this does for brain and attention span. See:
https://goo.gl/Jd7QGK
http://goo.gl/Hxb3Sc
http://goo.gl/9CkU1K
http://goo.gl/NpbrmK

Brooke: In general, how can parents counteract some of the damage likely already done to children who spend too much time on screens?
Alan: Check these good findings and resources for suggestions:
http://goo.gl/nCMe5O
http://goo.gl/BPp7gF
http://goo.gl/7HWE6P
https://goo.gl/0kRwFt

Chapter 3
THEORY, METHOD, AND STYLE

How to Enjoy Worldschooling at Home

By Omaira Alam

"Traveling - it leaves you speechless, then turns you into a storyteller."
- Attributed to Ibn Battuta

My husband, Josh, is one of the best storytellers I know. He has this dramatic quality about him which both of our children - the little performers - have picked up. He knows how to change the tone of his voice, how to use a dramatic pause, how to engage the audience with his wit and sense of humour, how to play with words that string together into an on-the-edge-of-our-chair situation, and thrust you into fits of laughter or thoughtful pauses or keep you asking for more.

Around the dinner table, Josh shares stories of his childhood, of his life as a teenager in rural America, and of his travels while serving in the US Navy. Each story is filled with colourful characters and hilarious anecdotes about friends, family, and brothers-in-arms. The ones that really capture our seven-year-old's attention are ones about Josh's antics with his brother and cousins.

I am grateful that our children have this connection with their father and have memories building. I grew up listening to stories from my mum about growing up in newly-created Pakistan and all of her travels: how she turned over her packing crates and made them into small tables covered in bedsheets in her sparsely furnished apartment in England as a newlywed, how she worked in a factory nearby and picked up the local English dialect, how sometimes when she's really upset a bit of Scottish flavor comes into her speech because of all her Scottish neighbours in Glasgow, and how "back home" to her, for the longest time after settling in a Toronto suburb, was Glasgow and not Karachi.

That connection by Josh, my mum, and all good storytellers is like a thread that binds us together as human beings. Stories of their travels and experiences make us yearn for a place we have never been. But what if you had the chance to make it so you, your children, your whole family could travel, experience and make memories to last a lifetime? More than a postcard, these experiences are priceless.

> *"I urge you to travel.*
> *As far as much as possible,*
> *Work ridiculous shifts to save your money*
> *Go without the latest iPhone.*
> *Throw yourself out of your comfort zone.*
> *Find out how other people live*
> *And realise that the world is a much bigger place than the town you live in*
> *And when you come home*
> *Home may still be the same*
> *& yes, you may go back to the same old job, but something in your mind will have shifted.*
> *And trust me*
> *that changes everything."*
> *- Anonymous*

When my husband and I got married, as a military family we knew and prepared for frequent travel. We understood that we would be travelling every two to three years and some of it to other countries. After thirteen years of service, my husband left the Navy and we became civilians ready to lay down some roots in the Valley of the Sun in Arizona, USA. It lasted almost four years till we uprooted ourselves and travelled cross country to prepare for a life of travel yet again. Every two to three years we will be living in a different country around the world.

> *"Not all those who wander are lost."*
> *- JRR Tolkien*

They call it wanderlust: the continuous desire to travel. Since my son was a toddler I've travelled with him everywhere and know that he has a deep, and strong desire to travel. He loves it and thrives on it. My two-year-old daughter is not far behind. Most recently, I took the two of them with me on an across-the-world trip to Australia. My son met his pen pal and forged a lifelong friendship. For me, it was an experience of a lifetime - both exhausting and exciting.

Travelling with children, although exhilarating and adventurous, is not possible for all homeschoolers. One of the key tenets of homeschooling is living life, not just reading about it.

> *"We travel not to escape life, but for life not to escape us."*
> *- Anonymous*

Worldschooling takes that to a whole new level. It takes you out of your comfort zone, forces you to find value in a different perspective, and learn through immersion. It enriches your experiences because it requires you to embrace the world with all your senses.

While there are families of homeschoolers that packed up for a year or more and became what is known as worldschoolers, it takes a significant amount of sacrifice and resources of time and money. With many homeschooling families already on one income what then is the next best option for those who need to stay close to home?

Similar to what is considered a "staycation" worldschooling from home is a close second to the actual experience of travel. Worldschooling from home is about an attitude and appreciation of the beauty of where you live. Immerse yourself in your local community by embracing these five tenets:

1. Never stop exploring your surroundings
Living in one place for many years we sometimes forget to "travel" to our local landmarks or experience the reason we were attracted to our current home in the first place. Make it a point to step outside your neighbourhood and explore the hidden treasures right at your doorstep.

2. Learn a foreign language as a family
One of the best ways to learn about the different corners of the world is to learn a new language. Every language reflects the culture in which it was developed and will allow your homeschooling family to get a glimpse of another culture.

3. Learn to cook a diverse array of foods
Take a cooking class as a family. Have a food competition or have a community cook-sale where neighbours get a chance to sample foods from all over. Even more fun, find someone in your greater community to teach your family how to cook a special dish from their culture. While a delectable experience for the palate, the greater experience of history and tradition from a living storyteller and chef will be immeasurable, especially if taught by an elderly person who has a lifetime of stories to share.

4. Use community mapping and historical mapping to learn about the not-so-apparent diversity in your local neighbourhood
Consider who was here before you and your family. Learn about them. Learn about how your local community developed: who came first, why? How was the city designed, why? Ask yourself these questions. Become a part of the story of your town by sharing your story with neighbours and community members.

5. Within your network of friends set up state-to-state swaps and/or province-to-province swaps
Share trinkets and other items from your home state or province with other friends to their home states using the postal service. This is a step up, like pen pals. Or keep it simple and have regular postcard swaps. There are also many companies that provide opportunities for adventure right from your home. One such company, Little Passports, offers USA and World Editions to have monthly packages delivered to your home about places around the world. Also check with the tourism and trade websites where you can have maps and brochures delivered to your home for free or for a nominal cost.

While these options aren't the same as worldschooling, they are definitely a step towards developing a bit of wanderlust in your children. They are also ways to develop the skills toward learning about your communities and the communities in which your children may eventually live.

The goal of worldschooling is more than just travelling for the sake of travel. It is a chance to learn about our global human family. It is a chance to learn about all the species we share this planet with. And ultimately it is about knowing Allah, through knowing His beautiful creation.

> *"And among His Signs is the creation of the heavens and the earth, and the variations in your languages and your colours: verily in that are Signs for those who know."*
> -Quran, Ar-Room: 22

While some of us may be able to do this firsthand, many of us can still experience the wonder, the awe, the immersion, while being at home. In the end, as homeshooling families we want our children to be the narrators of their own stories. We provide the opportunities, the places in the heart for memories to be made, whether we do it from home or from the mountaintop in the Himalayas. The stories our children tell will be different from ours because their time is different. We imbue them with the skills to become the master storytellers of their time.

> *"Let me touch a tree, smell the rain, see the sunset and hear the birds. Then when I read and write those words, I will understand what they truly mean."*
> - How We Learn

And, if we really think about it, are we not all worldschooling, merely travelers here for a short time? We hope to leave behind our stories - sweet memories - with our children who pass them along to theirs and so on, by the will of God.

> *"Live in this world as a traveler, and leave behind you every sweet memory. Indeed we are guests here, and every guest must soon leave."*
> - Imam Ali (RA)

One Teacher Finds His Calling in Homeschooling

By Khadijah Hayley

Homeschooling has become a controversial, yet surprisingly common, occurrence. In the United Kingdom alone, it is believed that between 20,000 and 100,000 children are educated from home as opposed to attending school. A phenomenon that was once met with raised eyebrows and interrogative questions, it is slowly becoming an acceptable choice in the hands of parents. Whether in an institution or a living room, the education of a child is an inspiring and essential component of life. Yet teachers, both professional and parents, often find themselves the subject of criticism as opposed to receiving the praise and admiration their job deserves.

Samson Ahmed is a secondary science teacher working in the Middle East. Initially from the UK, he chose to be a teacher out of a desire to inspire children towards education. He came to this realisation when asked to speak to some children at his friend's recreation centre.

"In my upbringing, education was standard; you get educated and you go on to University. I just assumed that everyone else was like that, but when I got talking to these kids, they didn't have aspirations like that. As far as they were concerned, some of them were going to copy some of their mates in gangs. I thought, 'No, there's another way, guys.' Talking to them, I would see them have this realisation and something would click in their heads, that actually, yes, there is another way. I thought maybe I could do something similar on a bigger scale and inspire children to have better futures."

Although a lot of teachers have similar epiphanies and start their careers inspired and enthusiastic, the world of education often becomes an uphill struggle. According to the International School Consultancy (ISC), 18,000 teachers left the UK to work abroad last year. On top of that, a YouGov poll showed that more than half of all teachers in England are thinking of quitting in the next two years. What is causing teachers to practically flee from their profession in search of something better? When asked what the biggest challenges were for a teacher, Mr Ahmed had a surprising response. With such a question, it is expected to spark a discussion on student behaviour and engagement. However, Mr Ahmed found a much bigger challenge obstructing his vision. The management of schools, whether on an individual basis or nationwide, often make the task of educating children rather difficult. "They [management] have certain ideas that may not be conducive to what I need to do on the ground. [....] I think, to some degree, they are okay at getting information about what [the children] need. But I think sometimes the problem comes when they make decisions about what to do with that information."

With challenges such as these, it is understandable why so many parents are choosing to pull their children out of the school system and nurture their education from home. In his experience, Mr Ahmed has had the pleasure of privately tutoring some homeschooled children. He noticed a slight difference in the way the students learnt as opposed to children in school. In general, he found the homeschooled children to be quite sharp, although they required regular breaks and changes in activity. "Because their study area also tends to be their living and playing area, it may have had an impact on their periods of concentration; it took a while to get some of the homeschooled kids to focus for long periods of time." When asked if this observation led him to believe that school children were in a better environment, Mr Ahmed was quick to clarify his point. "When [the homeschooled] children were on, they were a lot sharper than the school children. The school children may have been able to stay on task for longer, but I don't know if they were as engaged as the homeschooled kids. They were well into an activity straight away and to be honest, on the whole, I found them to be a lot brighter. Maybe they needed more stimulation and that's why they needed more breaks."

Interestingly, Mr Ahmed's wife homeschooled their eldest son whilst they resided in the UK. "One of the factors that lead to that decision was certain things were going on at school that, as a parent, we didn't really agree with. Kids were exposed to things that we didn't feel they should be, at least not at that age. So in terms of protection, [homeschool] was an option. We're not the only ones in that situation."

With this in mind, one must wonder what power an individual teacher has to protect the children in class from the same exposure they would protect their own children from. "It depends where you are," says Mr Ahmed. "In places like the UK, if you don't fall in line with policy, you will be reprimanded. So I suppose it's about deciding if you want to be in the UK and have to do it or other countries where you don't."

In light of the recent decline in the quantity of teachers and the quality of education in institutions, there is a lot of speculation as to what the future holds for the school system. "Maybe this is my own warped view," admits Mr Ahmed, "but there is an analogy drawn between [being a teacher] and that of an army because you are fighting against certain things [...]. I'd like to see people pay more attention to teachers there on the frontlines. They are the ones who have an intimate experience and intel as to what's happening on a daily basis. I think if policy makers pay more attention to what teachers are saying and experiencing and suggested solutions, then that could improve the situation for the children."

When it comes to schooling, or unschooling, the investment in our future is full of decisions that must not be taken lightly. It is clear that the education system is on the brink of change. The situation, in its current state, cannot continue. Whether we will witness a revolutionary shift in the management of school institutions, or whether homeschooling will become the new norm, it is clear that times are changing. Parents and teachers alike are taking the education of our children into their own hands.

"Aha!" Moments: The Hidden Blessings of Unschooling

By Sadaf Farooqi

Like everything else in life, homeschooling has its pros and cons. When most parents start off on this experimental journey, they usually do not know what to expect, except perhaps, the unexpected. Parents who have deeply and insightfully studied homeschooling, and have taken the decision to adopt it for their children as a conscious choice that they believe to be the best option for their upbringing, come to know that this route that they have taken in life can have many unexpected twists and turns, simply because there are no pre-set rules, requirements, or results. Homeschooling is a methodology of children's learning whose outcome and result depends greatly upon the unique circumstances and particular personality set of a family. There are no guarantees, no tried and tested milestones that they can be sure of. Change and dynamic adaptation are the most constant parts of homeschooling. The parents learn and grow as leaders and mentors themselves, once they commence homeschooling and as the years pass.

As an unschooling parent since 2011, I can vouch for the fact that unschooling has not always been an easy ride. It is that branch of homeschooling that is perhaps the furthest removed from contemporary schooling methods. Unschooling typically involves letting a child follow their interests, naturally, and does not involve any force, coercion, or structure in their individual learning. The child decides what they want to learn, how, and when, and the adults just supervise and facilitate their learning, from a distance. Consequently, there are many apparent "delays" involved in the unschooling journey, i.e. when a child does not accomplish something related to academics or development that the parents desire to see them achieve. This is when the parents have to have faith that, when the time for Allah's qadr (decree) arrives, their child will achieve a milestone that other school-going children their age have already traversed. However, and many homeschoolers will corroborate this fact, when the particular milestone or "Aha!" moment finally does arrive, it usually does so quite unexpectedly, and heralds the most pleasurable feelings of delight and surprise - for everyone in the family!

As an unschooler, I have received more than my fair share of negative feedback and criticism from people, strangers as well as relatives, about this choice - feedback that stems mostly from ignorance and doubt-fueled skepticism. Granted, unschooling is a pill that is difficult even for some seasoned homeschoolers to swallow, but it is also one of the most rewarding choices that informed parents could make. How?

Below, I share a few of the immensely exhilarating surprises that were in store for our family, which occurred solely as an outcome of our decision to unschool.

Early maturity

I had always read that homeschooled children matured earlier, mentally and emotionally. Even so, I was not prepared to actually see - with my own eyes - how quickly my children, particularly my eldest daughter, would mature.

It happens almost in the blink of an eye, or overnight. One day, your child is talking like an adult, and understanding mature concepts and theories quite a few years before reaching puberty. One fine day, they are too old to be interested in "babyish" activities and toys that they once found so enticing. Even though their young physical age still makes them gravitate towards a select few "kids' stuff", by and large they quickly prefer the company of adults in social settings because of their advanced maturity of thought and superior mental ability to grasp realistic ideas related to practical adult life.

Willingness to help out

Sad to say, I had been one of those youngsters who avoided helping her parents out in household chores. I would do assigned chores such as washing the dishes, or laying the table, a tad reluctantly. My incessant school studies such as homework and exam preparations provided a convenient excuse not to contribute at home unless a harsh scolding came my way. Before the age of twelve, however, my parents had not even expected me to provide a helping hand around home at all, unless to fetch something trivial from another room.

This is not the case with my unschooled children, alhamdulillah. Even before they hit age seven, they had started to willingly contribute to the household chores, albeit a little amateurishly and clumsily. The simple reason? They just did what they saw adults doing. It is amazing how much children learn just by observation, and will do what you do, instead of what you say. Whether it was readily mopping up a spill on the floor, or cleaning up after themselves by picking up the toys or throwing out the trash, the willingness with which they did it was certainly a very pleasant surprise to behold!

And their skills just got better with time. Good for me, eh?!

Giving worthy advice during family *shura* (consultations)

In lieu of the first point above regarding the early achievement of mental maturity, correctness of belief regarding the life of this world, and correctness of thought, combined with being in touch with reality instead of being lost in a self-centered 'bubble' embodied by the sequestered world of school work, friends, and academics, homeschooled children give surprisingly good advice and suggestions during family meetings and conversations.

Please remember that my older two children are eleven and nine years old, so receiving a worthy practical tip or advice as contribution to a family discussion from a minor who is not yet twelve, which actually offers a plausible solution to a challenge being faced by the adults, is quite enough for even the most ardent unschooling parent to be completely caught off guard with surprise!

Case in point, when our firstborn remembers the name and location of a certain store or shop that offers the right product that will meet our needs, or our second-born suggests a shorter route or road as an alternative to the one we have taken, which will enable us to reach our destination sooner, we parents instinctively know that something was done right when these sharp-as-tacks children were not sent to school!

Not retaliating to bullying

As unschoolers, one of the most common points of criticism and concern that we receive from people, is the issue of how our children will learn to socialize with others. Granted, when we started out on our unschooling journey, we also had similar concerns. It is only by the grace of Allah that our fears and doubts were put to rest over time. For starters, I am not a big fan of the "social skills" of school-going children in the first place. Whichever social class they belong to, I have observed how many school-going children socialize only with their friends, and tend to completely ignore others, even adults whom they know. Their friends form their entire world, with gadgets and useless past-times forming the 'gel' that holds these flimsy friendships together.

As for my unschooled children, as they grew a little older, they began to show admirable social skills in public, with a dignified demeanor that struck an optimum balance: they did not always desire to be around "cool" peers in order to have someone to talk to or hang out with, nor did they remain so shy and aloof if and when someone - anyone - tried to be friendly with them, that they'd freeze with fright or awkwardness. Their social interactions displayed a nuanced but guarded friendliness and respect that did not overstep any boundaries of social decorum and etiquette, nor made anyone feel offended or uncomfortable.

Unbeknownst to them, I acutely observe their behavior in play areas at malls, parks, and other public places where other children are around them, sharing the same games and rides, in order to evaluate their unschooling progress in real-time situations.

A couple of the most pleasing milestone moments came when other children mistreated my children. Once, another girl bullied my daughter by threatening her with physical aggression (she even yanked her headscarf!), but my daughter did not retaliate, nor did my son, who was present, do anything to return the aggressive girl's negative behavior. They both let it go by remaining cool. At another point in time, teenagers surrounded my son as he played on one of the game consoles in the mall gaming area, with one of the teens playing a game on the console next to him. These older children swapped his gaming card (which still had some money on it) with their empty one. They did not know that I had walked up just then and was standing behind them, deliberately staying away to observe what my son did in response. Though he showed them his anger with his face, he did nothing to retaliate. It was just a card with some money on it, not worth a fight. Just like his sister, he let it go. His response was in accordance with his training at home: always retaliate to other's negative behavior with positivity.

This, however, is not what I have noticed among many school-going children. Aggressiveness in response to bullying - a tit-for-tat, stoop-to-their-low-level approach - is just one trait that marks their social behavior, in addition to a penchant for making die-hard friendships in exclusive cliques i.e. going to extremes in forming both negative and positive social relationships. Our Deen, Islam, teaches us to maintain the optimum balance in social relationships, with family being top priority at all times, and alhamdulillah it has been a pleasure to observe that unschooling had subconsciously helped us achieve just that.

Expertise in technical and human matters

Last but not least, one of the most amazing results of unschooling, which I never expected at all, was the acute insightfulness and sharp observation that my children developed at around age seven to eight in figuring out the reality of things, people, and events in life. I was amazed to see how quickly they started to figure out the technical aspects of how gadgets, appliances, and other physical objects work, as well as how deftly they began to detect, decipher, and understand body language cues from the people they interacted with.

It was amazing for me to be able to see them grasp the reality of things, of people, and of events in life at such young ages. I never expected the absence of school in their lives to enable them to tune in so finely to the subtleties in life! This hidden blessing of homeschooling was truly a "surprise gift" of sorts from Allah, akin to a secret treasure that we had not even known to exist. Ever since the older two surpassed age seven, they figured out how to operate a new machine or tool without even reading its manual, within minutes. They can also tell what a person in their company is thinking or feeling, by just observing the changes in their facial expression, tone of voice, and choice of wording. Of course, this gift allows them to adjust and change their behavior accordingly, in all situations. They are also experts at relating cause to effect in events that happen apparently at random in life, and are able to detect sincerity or deceit in the people they interact with, within seconds. All of this is actually the initial flickering of wisdom - a priceless blessing that I have repeatedly asked Allah to give to my children.

As our unschooling journey continues, I can only thank Allah for not only giving us the guidance to commence with it, but also the steadfastness to remain patient upon it. There were many times when the going got quite tough, when we seriously doubted ourselves, and wondered if we were making a mistake. But such challenging phases only made us stronger after they passed by, and imparted to us invaluable lessons in the psychology of early life learning. It was the unexpected gift of these surprise blessings in unschooling, however, which were the real crème de la crème of the entire journey so far!

One Student's Pros and Cons List of Homeschooling

By Faiza Rahhali

Pros
I don't have to wake up early in the morning.
I can study in my pajamas.
I can be with my family 24\7.
I can have my own study time.
I can have midweek sleepovers with other homeschoolers.
I can do stuff in the middle of the day while other kids are in school.
I can advance much faster than kids who go to school do.
I have more time in the day to read, which I have been doing a lot of lately.
I don't have to be stuck in a stuffy classroom with a bunch of kids.
I have a say in what I want to study.

Cons
I don't get to see my friends everyday like kids in school do.
I can be with my family 24\7.
I have more chores to do.
I get a little lonely when I go to the park during the day.
I sometimes have to do projects alone.

Wavering Between University and Islamic Studies

By Alexandria Potter

U
p until the day I received my high school diploma from the correspondence program I had completed a few weeks prior, I knew for sure that I was going to be a special education teacher. I had looked up universities and planned out the classes I would need to take. I had volunteered at a great school for children with special needs and at summer camps as well. I was right on track... until that day anyway. Suddenly, I no longer felt sure. The worst part? I had no idea what I wanted to do.

I knew two things: (1) I wanted to study the Islamic Sciences, and (2) I wanted to change the world, but those are pretty broad statements and they did not directly help me decide what to major in. I felt pretty lost at that point. I was conflicted about managing both my Islamic studies and secular studies. I was confused about how I ever decided that I could be both a special education teacher and a homeschooling mom, equally important goals of mine. I was also starting to worry that I didn't even want to go to college - I hadn't been in a public school since preschool, so I wasn't sure how that would be, I didn't want to be in school for that many more years and there are plenty of awesome and successful people who didn't go through college.

Nonetheless, I graduated from high school in February and registered for the summer semester at my local community college. My older brother and I went together. The week before the semester began my brother and I went to Tennessee for a week-long *Seekers Guidance* retreat. That was an amazing experience and it was during that week, after meeting Shaykha Zaynab Ansari, (who has three children, studied and taught the Islamic sciences and was working on her Master's degree), that my perception that college and Islamic studies weren't compatible was completely broken. I still wasn't sure that college was for me though or, if it was, what exactly I should study.

So I went to school that summer. My major was listed as Special Education even though I was pretty sure that was not what I was meant to do anymore. Overall I had a wonderful experience. The campus was lovely, my classes were great, and I loved college! That was my last semester though. I had no clue what I wanted to do and I just decided I wasn't going to go - not right now at least. That was back in 2011.

Toward the beginning of this year, my brother and I were talking, as we do every once in awhile, about what we are up to, our goals and things we wish we had have done by now that we haven't or would have done differently, and he shared that he really regrets not staying in school. We graduated from high school when we were fifteen years old, thanks to Allah of course, our mom's wonderful efforts and our competitiveness. We could be working on our PHds by now if we had have kept going but neither of us currently even have an Associate's degree. The thing is though, no matter how much I think about it, I can't really say I regret my decision. Would it be cool to be 21 with a Doctorate degree? Yes, of course. But I don't think I would have gotten to where I am today, had I stayed in college and I surely would not have had the opportunity to do all of the personal-growth exploring that I was able to do in the past four years.

That fall in 2011, I started studying Islamic Sciences online and even though I was only taking one course a semester I was focused. I was also thinking a lot about youth work after hearing about the existence of a job called "youth director" at the retreat we had attended. If you would have asked me what I was doing at that point during the retreat, I would have said that I wasn't going to school and I was going to be opening an Islamic youth center as soon as I could! I have continued teaching Sunday school and volunteer in youth programs when I can. That youth center hasn't actually happened yet, but it is something that I still hope to accomplish one day. Last year I was able to launch Layla Lights, an online, membership-based, Islamic educational program to empower young ladies, and also work on writing the first two books of an Islamic children's series I have planned. Additionally, I started my labor and postpartum doula training, which I'll be finishing this summer God-willing. Now I feel like I know what I want to do - for the most part, at least. I have my mission.

Last fall I got back into school, majoring in Mental Health and Psych Rehabilitation. Of course I am still learning about myself and what I hope to contribute to this world and to an extent, I'm still a little dreamy with my goals and the projects that I take on. I got accepted into a Mental Health program at school, am in the Honors program and I have a 4.0 GPA. I love my classes, and because I'm sure this is what I want to do and it is something I'm passionate about, I'm able and willing to give my 100% to my classes - even math, which is almost never my friend.

Although I don't regret my decision, there were many times throughout my journey to today that I felt like I should be going to college. There were times that I would spend way too much time researching different fields and different college programs. There are times, even today, where I do feel a little funny that I'm 21 and don't even have an Associate's degree (yet). I'm happy with where I am, though. I am content with the unfolding of my journey to here. I want to end this piece with three small advice tips for anyone who might be feeling any of those ambiguous feelings or may be parents of young adults going through these things:

1. Pray Istikhara. Ask Allah for guidance. Don't rush into things - especially not because that is what you think you should be doing or that is what everyone else is doing. Even when you feel like you're sure about something, ask Allah about it before jumping in.

2. Whether you get right into college or not, listen to your inner self and be willing to explore. Serve your community when you have the opportunity- work with different people, different fields, get as much variety as you can. It benefits the world around you and it helps you build

yourself and figure things out.

3. Be patient and don't be rigid. Try not to be all over the place, so as to avoid not actually accomplishing anything, but remember that nobody knows the exact path their life will take. If you notice a pull into something new or bigger than you had ever imagined or that you think you want to do but you have every reason why you just can't do it, give it a try. You define yourself - but every claim has an outward manifestation. Be true to yourself, whatever that means to you.

A Homeschooler's Hand in the Birth Campaign for Syrian Refugees

By Isra Arfeen

Dear Fitra Readers,

My name is Isra, I am 15 years old, and I recently fundraised for a wonderful cause which was the 'Birth Campaign for Syrian Refugees' along with the help of my family and friends. I would like to share my amazing experience with you.

As I am sure you are all aware, families in Syria were facing very harsh winters with no healthcare, food shortages, lack of basic amenities, and so many other elements making their lives even more difficult. For the Syrian refugees already struggling against hardships, the arrival of a newborn baby, which should be a time of joy, becomes a cause for concern and tears. The reason I got involved in the Birth Campaign project was because of when I thought of those mothers, I thought as if I were one of them. I imagined what they must have been going through struggling to find a safe, secure, and well equipped environment for giving birth and wanting their child to come into a loving and comfortable environment. So this was my motivation into wanting to help my sisters in Islam, and this was when I decided to get my family and friends to help me hold a fun day to raise money for expecting Syrian refugee women.

My homeschooling teenage group came up with the idea of holding a fun day, which would include a variety of stalls and activities, such as games, food and drinks, arts and crafts, bric 'n' brac and much more. During our planning we had an initial target of raising £1000 overall including the money on my I Help Give page, but Alhumdulilah by the Mercy of Allah (SWT) we managed to exceed our target by miles and raised £2560.83! Some humble advice I would like to share with you all is that when you intend to do something for the Sake of Allah and you feel that it will be a great big challenge, or that you may not be able to cross this bridge on your own, just remember that Allah (SWT) will be a helping hand for you every step you take in your journey for Him.

Through helping the Birth Campaign, Islamic Help will now be able to build a maternity hospital to provide for expecting mothers and for their deliveries with equipment such as beds, medicine, after care, sanitary towels, baby clothes, food, and more. All of these are essentials which some of us may take for granted, and which we are blessed with, yet these mothers are truly struggling to find. This is how we as the Muslim ummah came together, to aid these mothers providing them with help, equipment, and essentials that they needed to ensure that they will In sha Allah have a safe and clean birth. As our beloved Prophet Muhammad (SAW) said in this beautiful hadith "None of you will have faith until he wishes for his (Muslim) brother what he wishes for himself". *(Bukhari)*

I would like to be able to continue to help as many of these mothers as possible, so that their newborns continue to arrive into this world in a safe, loving, and caring environment. May Allah (SWT) reward everyone who has helped and is yet to help with the highest place in Jannah, and may all those mothers who we have raised money for remember us in our time of need. Ameen

If you can, please donate to the link below:
https://goo.gl/hkgV8C

Thank you for your help and support,
Isra

Chapter 4
OUR FAVOURITE RESOURCES

Curriculum Review:
BEarthschooling Institute

By Chantal Blake

Warmth. Play. Celebration. Connection. These four words were my introduction to Waldorf education. I wasn't looking for or even interested in the work of Rudolph Steiner, but the fruits of his philosophy so beautifully presented in the Rhythm of The Home quarterly magazine caught my attention and reeled me in. The emphasis of rhythm and ritual seemed intuitive to me. As Muslims, we are constantly cycling in one orbit or another. The sun's cycles indicate the times of our daily prayers, the moon's phases inform our religious calendar, and our symbolic circumambulation around the Holy Ka'bah reminds us of our unified revolution around the center of our lives - Allah, subha'nahu wa ta'ala. Our plentiful rituals in devotion to God are the form of a greater substance and this is the kind of comforting, purposeful, orienting posture that Waldorfers articulate so well. The elements that repelled me from Waldorf were the fairies, solstice celebrations, and pagan holidays but by the gentle introduction of Dr. Kristie Karima Burns, founder of BEarthschooling Institute, I better understand the essence of Waldorf and how to adapt its principle into our lives as a Muslim, homeschooling family.

The BEarthschooling Institute succeeds at offering families the necessary tools to incorporate and embody the touch and feel so uniquely evident in Waldorf schools. The captivating stories, imaginative songs, productive activities, and wholesome recipes are organized for gradual interaction into your daily, weekly, and monthly schedule. The generic annual schedule follows the Gregorian calendar, inclusive of Western secular and religious holidays. However, BEarthschooling offers an impressively diverse array of cultural enrichment supplements that span continents, nationalities, and faiths.

The Islamic Waldorf supplement reorients the entire curriculum with Islamic cosmology at its core. Themed lessons are centered around the Islamic calendar and the historical and spiritual significance of each month. Fairies are omitted in place of jinns, nursery rhymes are reworded for Muslim children, and stories draw inspiration from the Quran, Hadith, and Arab mythology. As a second language, Arabic is integrated in teaching supplications, writing, and song. Craft activities are connected to important events like Hajj, virtues like generosity, and Prophets like Sulayman (alayhi salaam). The woven storytelling through it all makes the curriculum orally rich in the absence of texts and books.

Beyond the academic and cultural foundation, BEarthschooling Institute also offers curriculum for Wildlife Education, Naturopathy, Nutrition, and Herbal Healing for children. For families who make regular use of alternative medicine, these courses can help a child confidently learn and practice the many modalities that Allah has given us through plants, nutrition, and healthy lifestyle habits to improve our well-being. For mothers who want to immerse themselves in learning, there are also accredited courses and certification programs in Wildlife Education, Naturopathy, Unani Tibb, traditional Avicenna/Islamic medicine, and Eurythmy for Healing, an expressive and therapeutic movement art made popular by Waldorf schools.

The work of Dr. Burns is comprehensive and thorough. Her first-hand encounter with Islam and Muslim cultures helps to carve a space for Muslim homeschoolers in the world of Waldorf. The breadth of her institute's reach and scope respectfully accommodates a diverse community that can both learn and benefit from each other. She consistently invites feedback, ideas, and photos to be integrated into her website while engaging participants personally and personably. The homeschooling community she cultivates is truly international and can be a resource for your own family's home education journey.

Curriculum Review:
Oak Meadow

By Shannon Staloch

Waldorf curriculum has always had a pull on me. For years, I used another Waldorf curriculum. During the summer, I would pore over its pages, both excited and admittedly, a little overwhelmed by all that was ahead. Chalk drawings, form drawing, knitting, and drawing were all skills required of a good Waldorf teacher, and sadly, I possessed few of them. I tried though. With two littles underfoot, we did circle time, skip counting our times tables, form drawing on our chalkboard wall, and it was beautiful. It was also totally overwhelming.

Finally, I decided to try Oak Meadow. Die-hard Waldorf homeschoolers, turn their noses up at Oak Meadow because it isn't "true Waldorf". Maybe, but it is one good curriculum. I have used the kindergarten and fourth grade curriculums so far. These are solid curriculums designed for homeschooling families. Each week is laid out as a Lesson, within which are the various subjects, depending on the grade. Every craft, story, and experiment is simple and all contained in the materials.

For my fourth grader, the material is engaging and interesting. Everything from five sentence paragraphs to drawing perspective, to keeping a food diary and calculating the week's nutrient intake, has all been aimed at keeping learning self directed. For my kindergartner, we have worked on letters and numbers, and made lots of nature crafts. The lessons are short enough to teach from more than one curriculum, and for my older son, some are directed at him, so that he has to read passages, and all I have to do is discuss them with him. Ahh, so much better than wrangling with knitting, a skill I'd love to possess, but still don't. I do however, now have more time to learn, if I so desire!

Get Outside - With a Book or Two

By Klaudia Khan

Outside play is an essential part of childhood. It's not only important for physical health, but studies show that running wild in the park or garden encourages children's psychological and mental wellbeing. Outside is also the field of first discoveries and with some help and guidance we can seamlessly turn any trip to the park into playful science class. Here is a list of my family's favourite resources to encourage exploring the natural world.

For the little ones - up to 6 years old:
• OKIDO *My Big World*. We love OKIDO, playful and colourful books full of fun activities for the little ones. *My BIG World* encourages children to look closer at the world around them and explore it using all senses. There are lots of ideas for outside play and things to make and do and grow - such as mini garden in a jar. It's been a huge hit with my children.

• *Little Honey Bee* by Jane Ormes (Big Picture Press) is a beautiful lift-the-flap boardbook as well as a counting book, seasons book, and flowers primer. The little ones love to discover bees and other creatures hidden in the garden and parents get a chance to explain what bees do and why they are so important for the ecosystem. And the illustrations are stunning.

• Anything by Alain Gree, but particularly the *Nature*, *Seaside*, and *Seasons* books (Button Books) - these are wonderfully colourful introduction guides to the world around us. With beautiful images and just enough information to keep children interested and motivated to make their own discoveries. *Seaside* takes us on a trip to the beach where we can discover marine treasures and meet some seagulls, but first we need to get the suitcases ready! *Seasons* is a great first guide to the natural cycle of seasonal change and *Nature* is a compilation of both plus other Gree's books, showing different flora and fauna to be spotted in different environments.

• Classics by Eric Carle, such as *The Very Hungry Caterpillar*, *The Tiny Seed*, and *The Very Quiet Cricket* - simple stories sure to capture children's imaginations and allowing them to take a closer look at the everyday miracles of natural world.

For the age 5-7:
• *Nature's Day Out and About* by Kay Maguire (Wide Eyed Editions) is a lovely activity book and a follow up to *Nature's Day*, a book exploring the changes of seasons. Activity books are great for this age group and this one makes a good start with its colouring pages and spotting, crafting and collecting activities. It is beautifully illustrated by Danielle Kroll and appealing to young

children as well as a bit older - the upper border of seven years does not apply here. Some highlights from the book are: making ice art and a bee hotel, and learning to tell the difference between a frog and a toad.

• Little Collectors Activity Box: *Nature Art - Make Art from Nature* by Jenny Bowers (Frances Lincoln) - a great gift for budding artists to encourage exploring new mediums and for little collectors to show them how to turn their treasures into works of art. The box includes an activity colouring book, two frames, an envelope for scavenging finds and a poster. Some highlights from the book: colouring in a rainbow using things found in nature, making journey sticks, and exploring different ways of seed dispersal.

Age 8 and up:

• *Hello Nature* by Nina Chakrabarti (Laurence King) is a wonderful art activity, exploring nature through seasons scrapbook suitable for nature enthusiasts aged eight and over. Upper age limit does not apply here as I'm sure many grown-ups would find it interesting and inspiring. If you have ever come across the book Let's Make Great Art then Hello Nature is kind of similar in the way it explores the beauty of living things all around us and encourages you to capture this beauty through drawing, colouring, crafting, growing and writing poems. Some highlights: growing an avocado tree, learning about mushrooms, and drawing what you see on your horizon.

• *Outside. A Guide to Discovering Nature* by Maria Ana Peixe Dias (Frances Lincoln) - is my very, very favourite book on nature. It counts 360 pages filled with loads and loads of interesting information and lovely illustrations, it reads great and is full of ideas and inspiration. It contains a guide to recognize more than a hundred plants and animals, and an introduction to biology as well as weather, geology, and the night sky. If you are going to buy only one nature book, I'd recommend this one. It tells you what clues animals leave that could help us find them and why we don't always see the moon, what a tree is and why lizards need to sit in the sun, are there wolves out there and what is the sky made of. This book is great for the whole family, and I'm definitely planning to use it as my main science textbook for my daughters.

• *Nature Anatomy* by Julia Rothman (Storey) is a fascinating visual guide to the natural world. It is fully illustrated, and I mean illustrated by drawings not photos, and in a beautiful way showcases the nature all around us from the ground and below to the sky and above. In between there are lots of living creatures to discover and landscapes to name and weather to notice. There are some recommended activities, but the entire book is really like a big recommendation to go out and explore and then draw yourself, like my daughters and I did. And you can learn some scientific terms with the close-up drawings of the anatomy of a flower, a butterfly, a tree, a jellyfish, and many more.

RSPB Pocket Guide to British Birds by Simon Harrap (Bloomsbury) - how fun it is to watch birds? Well, here in the UK many people think it is lots of fun and so we have lots of great books to assist that. We have chosen *RSPB Pocket Guide* as it is the perfect introduction to recognizing the most common birds out there and it has beautiful illustrations which I favour over the photos.

- If you find that your family walks need some oomph why not try an outdoor scavenging hunt? *Gofindit* (Sensory Trust) is a brilliant nature treasure hunt game designed to encourage exploring outside with all your senses. There are 33 cards asking the players to find something red or something furry or something smelly or something wow. It's suitable for all the family and sure to make your usual walks to the park or a trip to the beach more fun. There are different playing options and flexible playing time. The game is published by Sensory Trust charity and available through their website as well as on Amazon.

Compilation of IT Studies Materials

By Klaudia Khan

But I Read It on the Internet! by Toni Buzzeo

Lauren Ipsum: A Story About Computer Science and Other Improbable Things by Carlos Bueno

Secret Codes & Number Games: Cryptographic Projects & Number Games for Children Ages 5-16 by Dr. Dev Gualtieri

Hello World!: Computer Programming for Kids and Other Beginners by Warren and Carter Sande

How to Code in 10 Easy Lessons: Learn how to design and code your very own computer game by Sean McManus

ABCs of the Web: Alphabet Primer for Young Developers in Training by Andrey Ostrovsky

Usborne *Lift-the-Flap Computers and Coding*

Web Design for Babies 2.0: Geeked Out Lift-the-Flap Edition by John C. Vanden-Heuvel Sr.

Ada Byron Lovelace and the Thinking Machine by Laurie Wallmark

Ada Lovelace, Poet of Science: The First Computer Programmer by Diane Stanley

Code Monkey Island - board game

Littlecodr - Kids Coding Game - board game

http://csunplugged.org/

Our Contributors

Omaira Alam is a mum of The Jibbers (7) and ZanyBaby (2) and has been actively homeschooling for five years with her husband, Josh Herald. She is the Program Director for the Islamic Teacher Education Program (ITEP), an online certificate program and a program of Razi Education. She is also helps Islamic schools develop a viable whole-community behaviour management model in partnership with Islamic Education Consultants in Australia, called Dignified Way. She holds undergraduate degrees in neuroscience, world history and global education from the University of Toronto. She completed her masters in Special Education focusing on at-risk students with learning and emotional disabilities from the George Washington University, and has almost 20 years of experience in education in diverse settings, and at various levels. As a regular columnist for the *Arizona Muslim Voice*, she also shares her musings about education on her blog, blackboardwhitechalk.wordpress.com.

Asma Ali is an avid reader, writer and dreamer who currently resides in KSA where she part-time homeschools her sons.

Zawjah Ali writes for Hiba magazine and blog, and other outlets. She has done her O and A levels and was halfway through my graduation in psychology when she got married. Zawjah is a proud mother of two Alhamdulillah. Writing is her means of contributing to society and to spread the word of Allah.

Isra Arfeen is 15 years old, a homeschooler with five siblings, and is currently studying for her upcoming GCSE exams. She is a freelance writer for various magazines, and enjoys writing and cooking.

Brooke Benoit is running her own private Sudbury-like school with her seven children on the southern coast of Morocco. She is an editor for SISTERS magazine, the founder of *Fitra Journal* and a writing workshop facilitator.

Chantal Blake is a writer and unschooling mom of two from New York City. She has lived with her family in different countries since 2008 and archives her stories and adventures at WayfaringGreenSoul.com.

Karrie Chariton is a homeschooling mom of three and blogger at http://www.theconvertlife.com. She helps converts discover the resources and support they need on their journey as Muslims. Karrie shares her experiences as a convert, which includes living in Muslim-majority countries for five years, and she also writes about being a homeschool mom in hopes of helping other Muslims who are interested in homeschooling.

Sadaf Farooqi is an author, blogger and freelance writer based in Karachi, Pakistan, who has been homeschooling her children since 2010. She has two daughters and a son. To date, Sadaf has authored over 300 original articles, most of which can be accessed on her blog, "Sadaf's Space". After her first non-fiction book on Muslim marriage was published by IIPH, and she has started self-publishing her past articles as non-fiction Islamic books, which are all available on Amazon and Kindle.

Khalida Haque is a qualified and experienced counselling psychotherapist who has a private practice, is a clinical supervisor, group facilitator, freelance writer and counselling services manager as well as founder and managing director of Khair.

Khadijah Hayley has just started homeschooling her two boys. In her own time she is a writer, editor and writing consultant. For updates on current services and e - courses, check out her Facebook page, www.facebook.com/khadijahhayley

Shaykh Ismail Kamdar is the Head Teacher of Islamic Online University, a BAIS graduate, Radio Presenter, founder of Islamic Self Help, author of multiple e-books and a homeschooling dad.

Klaudia Khan is a Muslim mum and writer living in Yorkshire, UK. She has three homeschooled daughters and loves to learn, create, and play with them.

After having traveled for several years, **Sumaia b. Michel** has settled with her two children and three step-children in Egypt. Having homeschooled all of her children, she has started her homeschooling consultancy Kenzy Unlimited. Besides consultancies, she writes Islamic and non-Islamic after-school programs and homeschool curricula. Always on the lookout to make learning fun, she often organises educational activities for her children as well others'.

Zakiya Mahomed-Kalla is an education enthusiast, and an aspiring linguist. She tutors Economics for the University of South Africa, and Arabic for the love of it. Some of her writing is currently on zakiyamahomed.com

Alexandria Potter is a 21 year old Mental Health major, aspiring student of the Islamic sciences, who is currently certifying to be a labor and postpartum doula. She is also a daughter to amazing parents and a sister of eight. She is preparing to officially launch the first book of an Islamic book series for five to eight year olds' called I Tell You I'm a Muslim. Please check out the program she recently relaunched, Layla Lights. If you'd like to follow her work, check out her blog or connect, you can stop by her personal website: http://alexandriawrites.wordpress.com/

ONLINE PROFESSIONAL DEVELOPMENT RESOURCE FOR MUSLIM EDUCATORS

ISLAMIC TEACHER EDUCATION PROGRAM

Transform The Way You Teach

learn how to apply Islam's timeless principles of teaching and learning in your homeschool

Join the mailing list for weekly educational resources & updates!
www.islamicteachereducation.com

BROOKE BENOIT
Homeschool Strategist

Assisting families in finding their educational goals and fit.

Contact for a consultation:
BrookeBenoit@hotmail.com

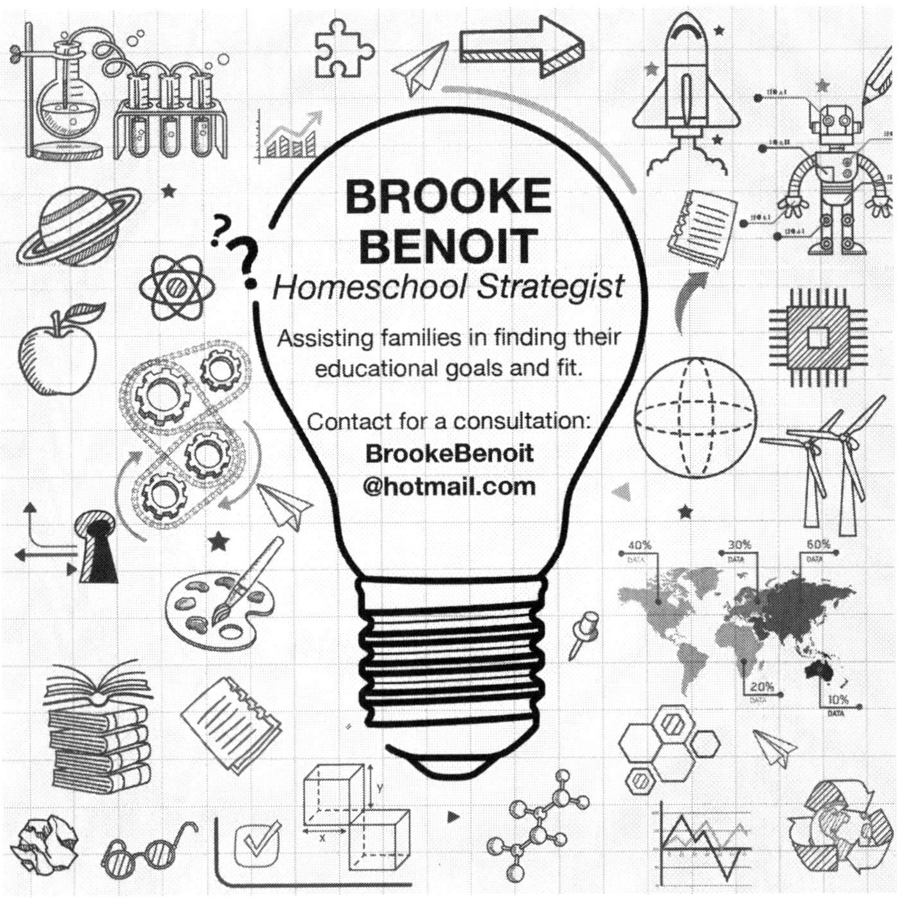

Homeschooling 101 is a guidebook designed for parents who want to learn how to start homeschooling and why they should do it. It is designed to help you settle into your first year of homeschooling smoothly.

Download today for only $6.99

http://payhip.com/b/NKpv

The Convert Life
WHERE CHANGE HAPPENS

HELPING CONVERTS DISCOVER THE RESOURCES AND SUPPORT THEY NEED ON THEIR JOURNEY AS NEW MUSLIMS & EDUCATING MUSLIM FAMILIES ON HOMESCHOOLING.

WWW.THECONVERTLIFE.COM | WWW.FACEBOOK.COM/THECONVERTLIFE
WWW.PINTEREST.COM/THECONVERTLIFE

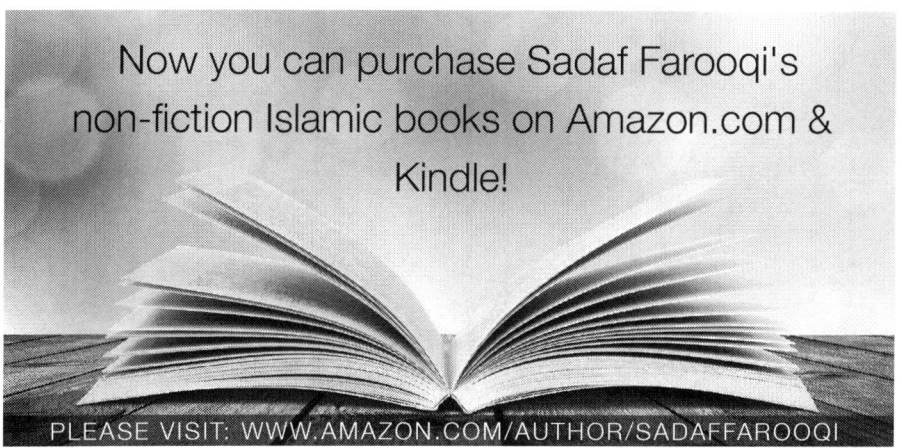

Now you can purchase Sadaf Farooqi's non-fiction Islamic books on Amazon.com & Kindle!

PLEASE VISIT: WWW.AMAZON.COM/AUTHOR/SADAFFAROOQI

Made in the USA
Middletown, DE
27 February 2018